Anti-Theist: /

By Christopher Mallard

Table of Contents

Prologue

**"There was
once a time
when all
people
believed in
God and the
church ruled.
This time was
called the Dark
Ages."
~Richard
Lederer**

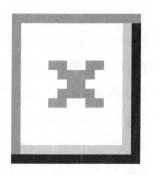

Hello. My name is Chris and I'm an anti-theist. My hope for this book is to help my fellow atheist/anti-theist in the intellectual battleground of religious debate that has sprung up over the past couple of decades. This new lease on life for atheism is in thanks, primarily, due to three things; the power granted us by the internet, the freedom of speech provided by our government, and the brave men and women willing to stand up and make the voice of reason be heard. Some of the names of my personal heroes would include Sam Harris, Richard Dawkins, Carl Sagan, and the late Christopher Hitchens, but there are many, many men and women around the world risking their lives to shine the light of reason. I certainly didn't invent this wheel we call atheism, I'm just giving it my own spin.

> **"If I were not an atheist, I would believe in a God who would choose to save people on the basis of the totality of their lives and not the pattern of their words. I think he would prefer an honest and righteous atheist to a TV preacher whose every word is God, God, God, and whose every deed is foul, foul, foul."**
> **~Isaac Asimov**

The advent of the internet and the almost unencumbered free spread of knowledge across the globe have pushed awareness of what it means to be atheist to a new level. People are given the opportunity to see the atrocities of their faiths LIVE as they unfold on television and this is driving people to question their beliefs. They are beginning to see it for what it really is, a lie written in books with peace on the cover but blood on almost every page. Many Bibles have a large cross on the front. One would think a book of religion with a large torture device depicted on the cover would be a clear indication of the content.

Another factor to be considered is that the internet has brought instant knowledge to the corners of the earth like never before and the overall IQ of the human race, for lack of a better term, and awareness of the vast peoples of the world has increased. The mass of the population is no longer an ignorant herd of sheep waiting to be told what to do. People are proactively using the internet to educate themselves and, put simply, they're not going to fall for it anymore.

In the past, if you were an atheist, you were alone and cut off from anyone else of reason when the voice in your head was telling you these crazy stories of gods and prophets couldn't possibly be real. Scared and oppressed, you would be silent, alone, and conform. But you should know you're not alone. The internet is full of free thinkers and, dare I say it, so is the world.

I find it amazing and appalling at the same time how so many intelligent people can follow such an obviously flawed belief systems to the point where they are willing to die or kill with no proof whatsoever that what they believe in is true or real. Religion is organized insanity at its finest.

> **"The word god is for me nothing more than the expression and product of human weaknesses, the Bible a collection of honorable, but still primitive legends which are nevertheless pretty childish. For me, the Jewish religion like all others is an incarnation of the most childish superstitions"**
> **~Albert Einstein**

This is a very special time for mankind. Never in history has the word of reason and logic spread so quickly and to so many. The second age of enlightenment for mankind is slowly passing and the dogmas and oppression it gave us will someday, hopefully, be completely banished by knowledge and understanding. The human race is finally trying to find its way through the darkness of the second age. From the inquisitive minds of our ancient ancestors who worshipped a burning disc in the sky, to their modern contemporaries who spend tireless hours in study and dedication to their faith, it's all nothing more than a misguided quest for understanding.

Unfortunately, some people ignore the truth and manage to suspend all levels of disbelief under the guise of faith, to the point of shaming their own intellect. One of my favorite quotes on the matter is as follows:

> **"Arguing with Christians is like playing chess with a pigeon. No matter how good I am at chess, the pigeon is just going to knock over the pieces, shit on**

the board, and strut around like it's victorious." ~Anonymous

So as you can imagine, until we stop indoctrinating our children with such foolish, hurtful, and hateful materials from birth we're always going to have those people who, no matter the amount of evidence or reason, will always be content to live in the dark.

And to that I say. . . Welcome, my friends, to the Third Age of Mankind. A true age of enlightenment where science rules and the dogmas of religion are exposed for the mythologies they are; little more than fodder for history teachers. Giving them the knowledge and wisdom to teach the coming generations about the horrors religion has wrought on mankind in order to avoid them in the future.

This book is intended as a satirical take on religion from an anti-theist viewpoint and there is some occasional adult language, so you've been warned. Get your crucifixes out and prepare yourself... here be monsters. When you look over the chapter headings of the book you can see I cover a wide variety of topics, each of which could be a book by itself; this is merely the opening salvo aimed at four distinct groups:

1. Atheist: With so many brave atheists openly proclaiming their lack of faith, it's very common for a new and unsure atheist to be confronted and browbeaten by a confident theist, and or face intense family and peer pressure to give themselves up to the religion. These brave people, often alone in their sphere, need as many tools as they can get to defend themselves, intellectually, when put in the position to do so by theists. If a theist asks you why you don't believe, show them this book.

2. Antitheist: Often times, an antitheist will find themselves in a debate with an intelligent, educated theist and can't remember the precise scripture that, for example, shows god murdering thousands of innocent people, or instructing you to kill your own children in the streets with rocks. I'll also be throwing in some pesky scientific facts which should also be of use to you, my fellow antitheist, in

your quest to save your fellow man from self-imposed mental slavery.

3. Theist: Have any doubts yet? If you're a true, dyed in the wool believer who has all the faith in the world that God exists and loves you, you may as well put this book down now. Some people simply want to be sheep. Most due to having been indoctrinated from childhood to believe the horrific fairy tale type stories forced upon their malleable minds by their ignorant, misguided, and sometimes malicious parents. Couple that with their fear of the unknown, or the fear of being different than the crowd, and you have a recipe for a flock. If you're tired of being a sheep and are ready to free your mind, this book is for you. As ironic as this may seem. . . let me enlighten you.

4. Agnostics: Is the sharp center of that fence you're sitting on starting to poke you in the butt? Purchase this book and ones like it to help fund the people with the backbone to fight for your children's right to not live in fear of the very religious oppression you now cower from. Visit your closest bookstore and pick out a spine that fits you and then pick a side... pansies.

Now listen, I'm not advocating you going out and brow beat every theist you run into. Don't be an ass! If you run into an 80-year-old woman in a nursing home, don't go ripping away her comfort blanket. Use a little common sense and compassion. Most atheists/anti-theists are also humanists. Some people you just can't save, and to try might be harmful. Use good judgment when choosing with whom you wish to debate.

And don't get yourself killed. I'm all about standing up for what you believe in, but I'm also a 'live to fight another day' kind of guy. We anti-theists are still a minority and the people we are speaking out against have a long history of being violent when confronted with a message of reason and logic. Use caution!

But I'm also a firm believer in natural selection. If you're foolish enough to carry this book into a mosque in the badlands of Afghanistan and start preaching against the existence of Allah, then hopefully you haven't already tainted the gene pool by having offspring. Clearly, you're not the sharpest knife in the drawer and I don't give out the title of 'Brave' to fools.

If by some twist of fate you should find yourself in a mosque anywhere in the Middle East holding this book you should be prepared to do one of two things:

1. Die in a very horrible and public fashion. If you're a fame seeker you might get lucky and have your stoning or beheading end up going viral on YouTube.

2. Throw down the book, curse it, spit on it, smack it with your shoe, set it on fire, then scream, 'Allahu Akbar! Let's go kill an infidel' and run out of the room.

    The only path to survival is '2'.

Now obviously there's a little hyperbole going on here; a spot of exaggeration, perhaps. I'm sure a great many Muslims will argue that their mosque in the Middle East is perfectly safe for such activities… and they may be right. I challenge them to prove me wrong, though. Get a sign that reads 'There is no Allah, ask me why' and hold it outside your Mosque and when they ask, give them a copy of my book. Winners or losers will be determined by survival rates. Good luck with that.

Before the tragedy of September 11, 2001, I never considered the dangers of religion. I believed in God and even thought someday I would be a 'warrior for Christ' but that didn't seem dangerous or harmful, because in my mind when the lord came I would have a huge sword and I would be killing. . . demons. Yep, that's the thought in my head. I thought I'd be killing fallen angels and sending them back to hell. Much to my surprise being a warrior for the lord is an ugly business.

"O Daughter of Babylon, doomed to destruction, happy is he who repays you for what you have done to us, he who seizes your infants and dashes them against the rocks." Psalm 137 8:9

The example being set for me is that I'm to feel happy as I murder infants? But wait, it's just a song, right? A song about vengeance and murder and teaches you it's ok to kill the children of someone who harms you. It's simply perverse to expect to find joy and happiness in the slaughter of children. Anyone's children! Out of context, you say? Go crack open the good book for yourself. Read Psalm 137 to discover what to do if a repeat offender drunk driver kills your children in a car accident. Go forth and joyfully find his children and murder them. Crack their bitty skulls against the pavement in front of their house. It's ok. God will reward you in heaven for your deeds and you should be happy. That's what the singer of the song is teaching. Suddenly the idea of going forth as a warrior of God doesn't seem so noble. I'm a relatively balanced individual, at least according to me, and I reasoned it out all by myself that this was an immoral way to act. But you know how it is. There are unbalanced people out there who read this crap and think to themselves, 'Well, if God says those babies need to die, then it's the will of God that they die.'. Unfortunately, all too often these same people take the cause upon themselves to see the deed done.

I also find it ironic that Christians are so against abortion, because every life is so precious, and yet they believe in a God who would not only order the murder of innocent children but then go on to brag about it in the Bible; his infallible word in which he brings enlightenment. They claim Christ changed the rules, but he didn't. The God of Abraham was a mean, vicious, and vengeful God, who by his own word admits to the slaughter or commanding the slaughter of millions of innocent people including children. Christ comes along and suddenly God is a nice, fuzzy, loving God? Really? Many Christians who read this will be nodding their head in the affirmative. 'Yes!' they will say. But why? In heaven, before the time of man, there was a war for the throne of heaven. In the times of the Old Testament, there were wars. Then Jesus comes along and says God loves you and if you believe in him, Jesus, you'll get into heaven. And subsequently, there have been wars in his name or against his name right up to this very day. Even the Bible says there will only be a few years of peace on Earth and that will be under the rule of the anti-christ, which I find ironic. Then God goes all Old Testament on our asses and the slaughtering really begins. All this murder, death, kill for what? Why? C'mon God! You're the almighty, can do any miracle, move any mountain, remove even the toughest stain, all-knowing freaking God! Ba weep grana weep ninny bon, already! Blink all of us non-believers out of existence quickly and painlessly then create a paradise for your believers.

"Science flies you to the moon, religion flies you into buildings." ~Richard Dawkins

But that wouldn't be any fun, would it? Why blink us all painlessly out of existence when he could take his time over a period of months, years to grind us screaming under his imaginary boot. Go read the book of Revelation where John describes angels being sent to rain fire and poison on the earth and then God calls forth these huge, hideous locust/scorpion things to sting, torment and torture the people of the Earth for months. Five months it says these things will ravage the people of the Earth with horrible stings but that the people will be unable to die. Then things start getting really ugly...

So it's nothing but war, pain, and murder from absolutely the beginning to the very bloody end, with three years of peace in which the anti-Christ rules the earth. Jesus himself doesn't murder anyone in the Bible, does he? Why yes. Billions of people slaughtered by the lamb who breaks the seven seals and releases damnation upon the earth. If it were a war and God lost, Jesus would be executed for war crimes for breaking the seals. Oddly enough at first, they couldn't find anyone in heaven, on Earth or under the earth capable of breaking the seals, and John claims to have wept and wept. Then they conveniently found the lamb. If the lamb was Jesus, then why did they have to look for someone to break the seals? No odd contradictions there. Back to the point, Jesus was the one pulling the trigger and literally murdering billions of people. Where's you're soft and fluffy messiah now?

In April of 2006 I was working in a small computer shop in Odessa Texas and one late afternoon I was having a discussion with the owner of the shop about the recent discovery of the gospel of Judas. I had heard about the discovery and that it claimed Judas was not the traitor everyone thought he was, while my boss thought it was at best a hoax and at worst the lies of a traitor. At the time, I was a skeptical believer and thought it made for good shop talk to debate the matter as an advocate for Judas. After an hour or so of my boss, a man of faith with extensive knowledge of the Bible, wiping the floor with me, I gave in. He had biblical knowledge on his side, but he seemed inflexible about the matter to the point where no amount of evidence would really even be considered. I didn't have the biblical knowledge to win the argument, but I was thinking I would prefer to wait for more scientific evidence before being so closed minded about it. Does the scientific information about the parchment or papyrus, the ink, the carbon dating all put it at the right time to be legitimate, etc. Maybe Judas wasn't such a bad guy after all.

Just then my brother came in the door. His face was ashen and serious and he asked me to step outside for a moment. Seconds later I found out my father had had a stroke. But that wasn't the worst of it. The reason for the stroke was due to 'dark spots' in his brain on the scan and they suspected cancer.

I was shocked. I walked back into the shop and explained the situation to my boss and he let me off so I could go to the hospital. There was this nagging feeling of, 'Did my arguing against Christ bring this upon my father?' and I've often wondered afterward if my boss had seen it as a sign from above for someone to argue against God's will and then have such bad news land upon them. But he was a pretty good egg and I doubt he felt that way. Either way though, the very fact I was thinking things so ugly, that perhaps my deeds had caused my father's cancer or that my boss would find religious right in the news, was just disgusting to me and I had to ask myself if that was a god I wanted to continue to believe in.

Well, turns out my father didn't have brain cancer. He had lung cancer. Stage 4 small cell carcinoma of the lung had grown and metastasized and traveled to his kidneys, his liver, and his brain. In the late evening of October 26th, 2006, he passed away. The cancer in his brain was very hard on him in the last couple of weeks and his mind seemed to come and go. His vision would fade and clear and he would see bright spots. His Christian life, his desire for something in the hereafter and his delirious state blurred the bright spots into angels... and they were waiting for him. And you know what? I didn't believe him. There wasn't even a debate in my mind about the subject. He was just hallucinating because of the cancer and his logical, yet deluded mind gave them names, form, and purpose.

My father wouldn't agree with the content of this book, but he would be proud of me for standing up and speaking out about what I believe and doing what I think is right. And so I dedicate this work to his memory.

I should note that three years after my father passed away from cancer it was discovered my former boss, the one from the debate above, had also developed lung cancer. He passed away in February 2013. He was a good man and a good friend. I would also like to dedicate this work to his memory as well, but somehow I doubt his family would appreciate the sentiment, so I've chosen not to mention his name... but he is remembered.

Chapter 1. What's the Difference?

"Atheism is more than just the knowledge that gods do not exist, and that religion is either a mistake or a fraud. Atheism is an attitude, a frame of mind that looks at the world objectively, fearlessly, always trying to understand all things as a part of nature." ~ Carl Sagan

Carl Sagan (1934-1996)

There are a lot of misconceptions about what constitutes an atheist. In the past four or five years since I came out of the atheist closet, as it were, I've had a number of different reactions from the religious people I've run into. One woman crossed herself upon hearing the word atheist and stepped back, but managed to regain her composure. I think it took her a moment to separate the word 'atheist' from 'Satan worshiper'. I can certainly understand as the two sound so much alike. At first, I fully thought she was going to run away, but then after a few seconds she said, "Oh, well, I go to this wonderful little church and I would really like you to talk to my pastor. . .".

In reality, a part of me was insulted. I knew she meant well and was worried for my soul, but what I heard was, 'You pathetic thing, you don't have any chains. I'm a slave and I love the chains I'm bound with. Here, let's go to the church, so you can try on a set of your very own chains.' In my own form of taking the high road, I kept those thoughts to myself, politely declined, and went about my way. That was one of my first experiences and at the time I was reticent about trying to remove the self-imposed fog from other people's minds, so I countered her attempt to convert me with a strategic removal of myself from the situation.

Another person asked me how long I had been worshiping the devil and if it had paid off. My favorite was when a young person asked me, 'So that means you're, like, one with the trees and stuff, right?'.

Once we get past the confusions of terminology, the first question I'm asked is what turned me from God. My favorite answer is. . . 'I've read the bible.'

> **"When I told the people of Northern Ireland that I was an atheist, a woman in the audience stood up and said, 'Yes, but is it in the God of the Catholics or the God of the Protestants in whom you don't believe?'" ~Quentin Crisp**

So, back to my opening statement, there are a lot of misconceptions about what makes an atheist.

The Merriam-Webster online dictionary gives the following definition of atheism:

1 *archaic*: ungodliness, wickedness

2 *a*: a disbelief in the existence of a deity

   b: the doctrine that there is no deity

I find it interesting that the very first definition is somewhat derogatory; falling back on the old Christian mentality of ungodliness meaning something bad or evil. The second example in the first definition is wickedness, which is even more concise in its disparity in the definition of atheism. A clear example of how even secular institutions can help, even if inadvertently, propagate the misconception of atheism as something nefarious. It also helps to answer the question of why so many theists mistakenly think atheist are immoral or worship the devil.

> **"No philosophy, no religion, has ever brought so glad a message to the world as this good news of atheism." ~Annie Wood Besant**

It's actually the second definition you should pay attention to, if you're truly looking to determine what an atheist is. Simply put, we don't believe in god; ANY god or gods. For an atheist, all gods, tall gods, short gods, fat gods, skinny gods, nice gods, and mean gods are nothing more than the imaginary conjurings of someone who didn't have the understanding and science to explain the things in this world that are bigger and more powerful than themselves.

Ok, so now that we've defined what it means to be an atheist, you must certainly realize if you don't believe in the evil, murderous Abrahamic god that drives the perpetual Judeo/Christian/Muslim blood bath and yet you believe in the ancient Egyptian sun god Ra, then you are still not an atheist.

The Egyptian Sun God Ra

If you don't believe in any of the thousands of run of the mill gods mankind has dreamed up over the millennia, but believe the universe itself is God and probably has no whim or care about humans, then you are a deist. The god/universe made everything, including you, but beyond that has no concept of you, the individual, whatsoever. If you imagine yourself as the god/universe you have no care or concern if one little bacterium in your stomach murders another little bacteria in your stomach. You are completely unaware of the lies that bacteria has told and how many times it masturbated, and when it dies, it goes to the same place all the pious, godly bacteria goes. A deist may also be an anti-theist in that they are against the religious cults that have done so much damage to humanity. They believe in a god/universe but they are likely to be against an organized religion based on a personal God the deist doesn't believe in.

A 'Theist' on the other hand, believes in one form of God or another who has a direct hand in the course of the life of the believer. 'A personal God', who usually lives in the sky and watches everything they do, loves them when they are good and smites them when they are bad. At best, judging them and making them feel bad about themselves. At worst, giving them a personal savior they are willing to die for, kill for, and who oddly enough seems to share the same value system as the believer. Often times, if a believer is going to a temple/church/mosque and the message being taught doesn't line up with that person's belief structure, they will continue to move from temple to temple looking for a God that thinks as they do; hates the same people they hate, etc.

At this juncture, I must point out there are many people out there who have 'found God' and have transformed their lives for the better. To me, this is a delusion and that person has just used God like a carrot on a stick to lead them from their drug addiction, or to help them get a job, or to be able to climb that mountain. The strength and will was in them the whole time, but something in their communal based psychological makeup made them feel like they couldn't make a difference or change themselves without some form of help. More than likely, it was because these people were indoctrinated from childhood but it never really took until they were adults and fell on hard times. Often, these people are at a breaking point in their lives and they turn to a support system that will help get them back on their feet, while at the same time giving them the attention a person down on their luck craves.

For the religious foundation in question, it's a win/win scenario. If they pour out some resources, i.e. help pay a couple of bills or connect the out of work soul with a church member who has a business and needs an employee, then they have made a small investment they hope will snowball. If that person continues to attend their church, they bring more resources in the form of tithes into the church over time, plus whatever free labor that person is willing to offer. If that one person brings his friends and family into the system, then the system will grow exponentially from that one small investment. This was especially good for the church back when Christianity was spreading through Rome. Convert the head of a household and he would make his entire family, servants, and slaves all convert with him. It must have been a very lucrative gig back in the day. Benny Hinn and other televangelists flying around in their private jets and dripping with money are excellent examples in the modern world that religion is equally lucrative today.

Almost sounds like a good thing, doesn't it? Well, it probably would be a good thing if it were an education based system rather than a system based on a religion that welcomes you with kindness, but worships gods and books full of violence, hate, bigotry, incest, pedophilia, etc. Once you take a large group of people, especially the poor and uneducated, and toss in a fervent belief in a violent, vengeful God, then it's just a matter of time before people start dying in the name of that God. Essentially, that friendly neighborhood church soup kitchen is little better than a terrorist recruitment center.

'Welcome! Here is some food. Eat and be warm while I tell you about a kind and merciful God who loves you, thinks you're special in his eyes, and wants nothing but the best for you.' And then they hand you a book that is confusing and contradictory and absolutely dripping with blood. It's amazing how through the sheer power of the intellect of man, and the unmatched ability of the human mind to deceive itself, these good-hearted people are able to take a horrible moral example like the bible and somehow fool themselves into believing it's actually a message of love, hope, and peace. The only hope to be gained from reading the bible is the hope that none of it is true.

"My goal is simple. It is a complete understanding of the universe, why it is as it is and why it exists at all." ~Stephen Hawking

Agnostic people are those who aren't sure. They're on the fence and don't know whether there is a God or isn't a God. This group of people is often held in slight contempt by both sides of the God debate for their unwillingness to 'pick a team', but theist and atheist alike also see them as a pool of recruitment candidates ripe for the pickings.

"Isn't an agnostic just an atheist without balls?" ~Stephen Colbert

After this quote, it's only fair that I point out my ex-wife was an agnostic and indeed she did not have balls. . . but I digress.

For simplicity, we'll go with this… when you are filling out a form and it asks if you believe in God, if you check the 'yes' box, then you're a theist. If you check the 'no' box, you're an atheist. If you check the 'I don't know' box then you're agnostic.

Ok, I'm getting a little ahead of myself here. My colorings of the terms used to describe the belief or nonbelief in God do seem a bit biased with a hint of anti-theism. Wait wait wait wait! Did I say anti-theism? Yep. Not the same as an atheist? Nope. Well, sort of nope.

Of course, if this book were written by a theist, it might read that an atheist should be considered wicked because even the dictionary says it's so. It might also read that an anti-theist is essentially a militant atheist and that we eat babies and worship Satan. I would argue that since we don't believe in ANY supernatural beings, Satan is just as much a fictional character as the evil God monster of the Old Testament. Eating babies is also a ridiculous assertion, but it was once an argument theists used to scare people, especially children, away from the very real threat a person of reason posed to their house of cards faith. People make these false claims as if they were valid and true and warp the perceptions of people who have never even met an atheist. Some argue we use logic and reason with wicked intent to lead your soul away from the light of Yahweh, Jesus, Muhammad, Thor, and the Easter Bunny. This is absolutely true and, if you're looking at it from the perspective of a theist, it is indeed wicked, because the intent is to lead you away from your imaginary god. Unlike theists who rely on a fairy tale book and a sword, we atheists feel reason and science are our most powerful weapons. Oh yeah, and sarcasm. We're very fond of sarcasm.

As a believer you may find it difficult to comprehend that when an anti-theist is trying to turn you from your faith, we feel the same way you feel when you're ministering to someone who isn't part of your religion. You care for their eternal soul and want them to believe the way you do so your God will be merciful to them after they die. We don't believe in souls. Rather, we believe you should focus on enjoying this life and being a good person for the sake of being a good person. This life is the only one we have; leave the best mark you can. Our intent is good. We see slaves bound by a master who doesn't exist. He was invented by a barbaric people living in barbaric times, so it's no wonder the rules and lessons we (humans) take away from their teachings are barbaric and have barbaric results. And by that same view, it's no wonder people of reason would want to abolish such things.

Sooo. . . what is anti-theism you wonder? Oddly enough, at the time of this writing, you won't find the term 'anti-theism' in the Merriam-Webster online dictionary but I will tell you.

Onward towards enlightenment. . .

Chapter 2. Anti-Theism

"When two opposite points of view are expressed with equal intensity, the truth does not necessarily lie exactly halfway between them. It is possible for one side to be simply wrong." ~Richard Dawkins

Richard Dawkins at the 34th American Atheist Conference in Minneapolis

There are some subtle differences between an atheist and an anti-theist and often, even in this book, you'll see the terms used interchangeably. An atheist doesn't believe in any divine creator or Supreme Being but they tend to be a 'live and let live' group and usually profess nothing more than a non-belief. Generally speaking, they don't proactively speak against religion unless it's forced upon them and they tend to keep to themselves on the matter. I would presume for most due to fear of persecution.

The anti-theists, on the other hand, has an active distaste for religion in its various forms and believes, to one degree or another, that religion is a bad thing; a veil of darkness which should be lifted from the eyes of mankind. On their most placid level, an anti-theist might take only a slightly more proactive view than an atheist's 'live and let live' policy and state that a theist should not be allowed to present their faith in public, and to not press it upon those who don't seek it, but they should, at the very least, be allowed to believe what they want. The far extreme wing of anti-theism would be for a very proactive purging of religion from society. Forbidding the teachings of any god/prophet/faith and recommending imposed psychiatric evaluations and deprogramming treatment for anyone who can't break their mind free of the chains of their self-imposed slavery.

> **"Tell people there's an invisible man in the sky who created the universe, and the vast majority believe you. Tell them the paint is wet, and they have to touch it to be sure." ~George Carlin**

Upon reading the end of that last paragraph, you may have found yourself appalled at the idea of forcibly forbidding the practice of religion and one's right to worship whichever God hates the same people they do. Get over it. For over two thousand years, and closer probably to four or five thousand years, the Abrahamic monotheistic murder machines have forced their beliefs on others in one fashion or another; most often at the point of a sword. It's my opinion, and thanks to the freedom of speech and removal of religious oppression I'm allowed to publicly express it, that the religions of the world should be banished and replaced with reason. You don't have to share or agree with my opinion, but I'm allowed to have it.

Anti-theism, again, in my opinion, would not profit at all by the use of the sword. Knowledge is the sword of the anti-theist and doubts in the ridiculous tales the theist has been told throughout his/her life are the chinks in the armor of their faith. The cessation of the indoctrination of children into cults that worship blood and death, coupled with a well-rounded, science-based education is one of the biggest weapons we can use against the barbarians at the gate. That's right! If you're a theist, I just called you a barbarian. In my mind, someone who shuns reason and embraces the teachings of ancient death cults is a barbarian.

Thanks to television and movies, everyone in modern culture can easily imagine a Satanic ritual with candles and hooded figures all standing around chanting; a big pentagram drawn on the floor with an altar in the middle and a woman, presumably a virgin strapped to the altar. The leader of the hooded group plunges a knife into the girl, the chanting growing to a crescendo as her life ebbs away. He then takes her blood and either drinks it, gives it to the others to drink, or just sprinkles it all over in general. He takes out her organs and starts handing them to the others who either eat of it or lay it at the foot of the altar. Remove the pentagram and replace it with twelve pillars of the tribes of Israel, replace the hoods with robes and turbans, and these are the people you're worshipping! Read the bible and look at the descriptions of the sacrifices and offerings and try to picture what's going on in your mind. It's vile and barbaric, even for the day.

You don't necessarily have to be an atheist to be an anti-theist, although most anti-theist, I believe, would also classify themselves as atheists. I have met theists who believe in a personal god, but don't believe in the religious establishment and feel it fosters harm to mankind, and by that description consider themselves anti-theist, but not atheists. To me, they're just one more subset of nutbag I need to teach my children to watch out for and avoid.

The followers of the bloodthirsty Abrahamic religions shouldn't be the only ones who feel somewhat insulted by the nature of this book. I can't really speak for all anti-theists, in fact I'm sure many Wiccan consider themselves to be atheist in that they don't believe in the evil God monster of the Abrahamic religions, but in my opinion if you worship the Earth and trees and plants and feel you can communicate with same on some kind of ethereal or supernatural level, then I just think you're nuts. Batshit crazy, in fact.

George Carlin (1937-2008)
Image courtesy of Associated Press

You either really believe that crap or you just want attention in an unusual way. Either way, I would recommend a psychiatric evaluation and enrollment in a four-year biology course at your local university.

To a degree, we as a society owe a debt to the Wiccan for the very real scientific and medical discoveries their conjurings have provided. Like Neanderthal is a brother of Homo sapien, Wicca is something of a brother to science. In my opinion, the reason they never advanced further than they did as far as the efficacies of their medicines and spells is because of their insistence on trying to attach a type of mysticism to the knowledge.

But again, another fine example of man's ability to do something that fails over and over again, yet somehow he has the capacity to fool himself into believing someday it will work. Einstein's definition of insanity. If Wiccan spells or voodoo spells or any of that crap really worked we would be doing it in hospitals. And this is all especially true for those of the Abrahamic death cults. If prayer is so powerful, then when you called 911 to report an emergency, why isn't your call directed to your local church? An absolute fact you can bank on is this. . . If you took two hospitals and put doctors and nurses in one and priests and nuns in the other and had both groups heal only within the means of their teachings, the difference in the survival rates of patients between the two hospitals would be staggering. Especially if all the patients going into the hospitals are known to have fatal but treatable illnesses to where without real medical treatment or clear divine intervention they would die. This would be proof prayer doesn't work in any measurable form. 100 go into each hospital but 85-95% come out of the science hospital alive while the religious hospital would require no wheelchairs, only body bags. Every time. . . regardless of what religious group of priest/nuns/imams/witch doctor is doing the praying. It won't matter. Every time, guaranteed. I doubt you could find a township or city that would be willing to let you try such an experiment.

But that's part of the point of anti-theism. We see the damage these religions have done over time and believe it's time to stop. Mankind is too smart for this. There was a time when the Middle East was a center of knowledge and where people went in search of understanding, but it has become a wasteland; destroyed by the wars of the followers of the Abrahamic religions. It shuns reason and embraces mysticism and barbarism. Its arcane message and lessons range from the benign and silly to the outright dangerous. Mix saliva (spit) with some mud and rub it in a blind man's eye and he will be healed? Jesus did it, so surely it must work. Hmm, a family of Idolaters moved in next door. How should I greet them? Let me check my trusty bible to see what God says to do with Idolaters.

"As I listened, he said to the others, 'Follow him through the city and kill, without showing pity or compassion. Slaughter the old men, the young men and women, the mothers and children, but do not touch anyone who has the mark. Begin at my sanctuary.' So they began with the old men who were in front of the temple. Then he said to them, 'Defile the temple and fill the courts with the slain. Go!' So they went out and began killing throughout the city. While they were killing and I was left alone, I fell facedown, crying out, 'Alas, Sovereign LORD! Are you going to destroy the entire remnant of Israel in this outpouring of your wrath on Jerusalem?' He answered me, 'The sin of the people of Israel and Judah is

exceedingly great; the land is full of bloodshed and the city is full of injustice. They say, 'The LORD has forsaken the land; the LORD does not see.' So I will not look on them with pity or spare them, but I will bring down on their own heads what they have done.'
Ezekiel 9:5-9

In the above scripture, the 'lord' has commanded the merciless slaughter of his own people; every man woman and child who does not bear the mark. God slaughtering the chosen people of Israel, right there before your very eyes. Examples just like this make the anti-theist proclaim that even if your God is real, which we don't believe and you have no proof of beyond the scribblings of a group of uneducated, STD-riddled desert worshipers, it's evil and we should be against it.

Atheists have temples of healing, they're called hospitals and our God, science, will heal you to the best of his abilities, regardless of whether you believe in him or not. You just have to show up. We also have temples of worship, they're called universities. Anyone can go there and learn the lessons being taught and they really work in the real world whether you believe in science or not.

Modern-day universities and centers of education should shun Creationism and Intelligent Design in all their various forms. These modern-day witch doctors want to try to pass themselves off as real scientists with real science, but in reality, they're nothing but charlatans using bastardizations of meanings and horribly twisted science to back up their claims. Any time there's a question science can't answer, they immediately look to God as the solution and stop the search for a true, scientific answer. This is terribly harmful and leads people away from the real truth.

See! We see it the same way you, the theist, see it. You want to stamp out atheism and save as many souls as you can. We want to stamp out religion and save as many people as we can. The difference is that we can prove there are people, the theist cannot prove there is a soul. We strive to enlighten people to the fact that they should live for the now. Be good and enjoy life NOW, because this is all we have. There is no evidence the afterlife the religions speak of is true, so why put all the effort, time, blood, shame, and money into going somewhere you don't even know exists? And based on the sparse descriptions given of heaven in the bible, would you really want to go there anyway?

> **"Religion is the sigh of the oppressed creature, the heart of a heartless world, and the soul of soulless conditions. It is the opium of the people." ~Karl Marx**

To be fair, these Abrahamic religions were not the only religions of the day. In fact, many of the stories of the Holy Bible are direct rip-offs from earlier religions, lending even more credence to the argument that it's all a load of crap and shouldn't be believed. You may think of religion as a harmless comfort blanket, but in reality, it is indeed the most pernicious weapon of mass destruction ever created by man. It's a self-imposed mental disorder that robs people of their families and their lives.

You are kidding yourself if you think your legacy will live on in heaven. It's your works on earth that will be remembered. Our species as a whole would be better off if religion in all its forms were banished. Every hour spent on bended knee or in a place of worship should instead be spent in the study of things of a non-religious nature, whether it be for scientific advancement or merely self-betterment. Every dollar given in tithe should be given to institutions of scientific and medical research. Do you realize that had religion not stunted scientific advancement so much, and had the principles I just listed been enacted, most of the prayers you are praying wouldn't be needed? If we had shunned religion and embraced science three thousand years ago, we would be so much more advanced, technologically speaking, than we are now. If you have a loved one dying of cancer, you should right now scream to the top of your lungs and curse all the religious nutbags who have used the boogeyman of their faith to suppress and hold back science. Although I'm a man who loves history, sometimes I feel that if it's ever learned without a doubt that Jesus died on the cross and was not resurrected, or that he never existed at all, then we should banish his name and the name of his followers from the history books. We should erase them from time as their punishment for the damage to humanity they have caused. And that goes for all of them. The only problem with this is that your descendants have to be warned, and therefore the history must be written. But all the characters of the Abrahamic religions should be seen as villains against mankind. Their names should rank among the vilest perpetrators of hatred in human history. Their images should be upon the wall of shame, high above other such monsters like Hitler and Pol Pot.

We need an atheist city, we'll call it New Atlantis for the irony of it, where science is embraced and cultism and religion are absolutely forbidden. We would dwell in this great city until we had the technology to terraform and colonize Mars. We could enjoy and explore the solar system. Capture asteroids and mine them for the precious metals, then build plexiglass-like spheres around the entire asteroid and give it an atmosphere and grow crops on it. Of course, the plexiglass-like material will have to be capable of blocking out most of the sun's harmful radiation, but it's not an unattainable technology. The possibilities are unlimited, especially when they're not fettered by the dogmas of religion.

The Earth is infested with religion and there's no humane way to remove the infestation, so those of us not afflicted should flee. Move to Mars and leave monitoring equipment on the moon and in earth orbit so we can observe and document the continued religion-fueled destruction of man on Earth. An unfortunate reality is that we would be wise to have laws against allowing people to leave earth while still burdened with religion. Quarantine the earth until the problem works itself out. However, our current level of technology was attained even despite the restraints of religion, so it's not unthinkable that once the people of New Atlantis migrated to Mars, the remaining humans would eventually advance scientifically enough to make a similar exodus. It's at this point I believe we would be well advised to prevent them from leaving and spreading their sickness to the stars. Thankfully that's a debate for future generations.

And by 'works itself out' I only see two options. Either they turn their backs on religion or wars of religion wipe out the remaining indigenous population. These wars may also be over a lack of resources, which could have been prevented by advances in science which were shunned or stunted due to religion. Another example would be a plague that wipes out the entire population when basic levels of research in stem cells could have found the cure, but religious mentalities held back or prohibited the research. A third option, of course, is that the humans on earth continue plodding along from one bloody atrocity to another for several thousand years.

> **"You believe in a book that has talking animals, wizards, witches, demons, sticks turning into snakes, food falling from the sky, people walking on water, and all sorts of magical, absurd and primitive stories; and you say that I'm the one who is mentally ill?" ~Dan Barker**

Oddly enough, this sounds somewhat familiar. What if the peoples of Atlantis, and other legendary or mythical cities, were actually the culmination of that era's atheists who embraced science and technology and got off this rock while the getting was good? That would explain a lot. Earth being deemed infested with religion and quarantined from direct contact would explain why we haven't had direct and public extraterrestrial contact. We do get lots and lots of reports of their probes and scientific research craft, if you believe that sort of thing, as they monitor and document the ongoing religious infestation of Earth.

I imagine the galactic news outlets were abuzz back in the 1940s, when the religion infected Earth humans were developing nuclear weapons and rocket technology. I wonder how many councils were convened by the peoples or races in our local galactic cluster to debate whether we should be allowed to continue to develop technologically. It would appear they followed an, 'it'll work itself out' line of thinking. Who knows, there was an abrupt halt to the advancement of mankind back in the 70s and 80s and there are conspiracy theories out there who would have you believe the major governments of the earth were warned to halt their advancement into space by an outside, extraterrestrial force. Could religion have been the reason? I don't know. Sounds like another round of douchebaggery, worshipping the star gods of Nibiru or some shit, until they can hook me up with some proof.

Religion, however benevolent on the outside, is clearly the most dangerous and insidious weapon of mass destruction ever created by man. It would not be beyond reason to think if there are more advanced civilizations monitoring us, they may very well have designs to keep us from advancing for that very reason. Although I don't personally subscribe to the teachings or beliefs of the conspiracy theorists, I have to tip my hat to them on their reasoning on this one. The space shuttle was designed back in the 1960s and 1970s and it's still the best thing we have? Touché, conspiracy theorists, touché.

We should consider religion-free zones. We already have them to a degree in public schools and public buildings, but that's just limiting the official sponsorship of any form of religion. We should really take this a step further and proactively ban the practice of religion or the displaying of any religious icons in these places altogether. Your psychosis and your little mini torture devices don't belong in my educational institution; they belong on the dust covered window seal of a mental institution.

The anti-theist movement is coming. Our weapon is knowledge and we tend to toss in a spot of sarcasm for free because we love you. So prepare to close your eyes, put your hands over your ears and go 'la la la la la' in defense. We'll let you call that your magic shield of faith. We should make signs to put on our doors saying 'You are welcome here, your God is not.'

Ok, enough of this, on to more interesting stuff. The following chapters will consist of power in the form of knowledge.

Be careful how you use it.

Chapter 3. Disproving God

"Yes, I do have proof that God does not exist. It's perfect and irrefutable. I'm not going to show it to you, however. You cannot see it or detect it in any way. You cannot deduce it from the laws of logic either. You might claim that I do in fact have no such proof. But you have no proof that I don't. Sound familiar?"
~Rune Friborg

God by Michelangelo Buonarroti
(1475–1564)

How do you disprove something that doesn't exist? In the case of an omnipotent God, I would maintain that you do so by observing the absence of any proof of said existence, the inability of the followers to manifest it in any form, or to back up any of its supernatural claims. It should be illegal to teach a religion until you figure out how to prove it, since religion is such a dangerous thing.

Ok, let's play a game. You have your personal God who follows you around and feels you are so important he's going to broker you with some of his undivided attention and time. That's awesome. It may not actually be him though; perhaps just an angel or two to watch over you while he takes care of the big stuff like watching a small child in Africa die of starvation, helping a young theist win his high school football game, or helping that hungry stockbroker buy or sell at just the right time. But regardless, in one fashion or other you have the might of right on your side. Deal, done, perfect.

Your God is all mighty, all knowing, and all powerful, but I bet dimes to donuts he can't knock this bitty little cup off my desk. Go ahead and ask him to smite my unholy Minnesota Vikings cup from my desk right now. I'll pick it up and put it back on the desk (or get another cup if first one is obliterated) and see him repeat the event just once and I'll be a dyed in the wool believer forever. C'mon, pray real hard. . . I'll wait. I promise the cup isn't nailed or glued down or nothing, so no tricks. Hell, it's empty, which is a shame in and of itself, and it's already cracked where the handle meets the mug so go ahead. . . smite away! We should have made a stipulation in the rules against the use of earthquakes and tornadoes, etc. C'mon he's God and he can do anything so let's see a little finesse.

> **"One might be asked, 'How can you prove that a god does not exist?' One can only reply that it is scarcely necessary to disprove what has never been proved." ~David A. Spitz**

Of course, you the reader and I the author both realize you can't possibly know the current state of my cup, since you haven't read this work as of right now (Tricky, I know, but stay with me). But you know what? If your God is real, then he does know. He's everywhere all the time and knows everything, right? So why isn't he knocking my cup off my desk? He loves me, right? Wants me to believe in him forever and all that stuff, right? Well, I'm here, the cup is here, God is. . . a no show. Alone in this room, he could prove to me once and for all he's real and I would believe, but it won't happen. There was probably a tornado poised right over my apartment ready to rip my cupeth asunder until I said no tornadoes, at which point it whimpered and slinked away all sad.

Ok, I get it. Your God doesn't jump through hoops just because I say he should prove himself. What a cop-out crock of mindless drivel. Your God will fail this simplest of tests every time. He's all mighty, ever present, and nowhere to be found. This works every time.

Oh, wait! I think I almost saw the cup move. . . nope.

Disproving God sounds like quite a challenge, but when you stop and think about it, it's really not. In the previous chapter, I mentioned the two hospital scenario where we use a hospital full of trained doctors and nurses and a hospital full of priest and nuns to not only disprove the efficacy of prayer verses real scientific medicine, but as a happy coincidence, it also disproves the existence of God. Of course, it's not a complete one-off. You couldn't simply do it once with, say, Catholic priests and when they lost proclaim there is no God. No, you'd have to go through each and every sect of every faction of every nutbag religion pitting their best seers, priest, mullahs, leeches, imams, and witch doctors against Harvard Medical's finest. Then, when you're done and they've all lost, you can proclaim there is no God.

> **"You can't just say there is a god because the world is beautiful. You have to account for bone cancer in children."**
> **~Stephen Fry**

The horrifying reality of it is that if the religious fanatics of the world ever got it in their heads to try the above experiment and had the authority to do so, they would happily go through each religion until they found one that worked, thousands upon thousands of sick and innocent people would die slow and painful deaths in the attempt, and in the end, since there is no god, we would be right back where we started.

Regretfully, due to the loss of life in the lesson, the Muslims are giving us an excellent example of a different version of my disproving god hypothesis across the Middle East now as Sunni and Shia Muslims rent each other asunder in the name of Allah. It would appear to be a popular belief that had you been worshiping the right God, or in the right way, then surely he wouldn't let me kill you and your whole village, but since he did then clearly you were doing it wrong.

It's God's lack of action, not his actions, that disprove his existence. If prayer really worked, there would be groups of theists (nuns, priests, imams, whatever) going from bed to bed in every hospital healing the sick. Of course, there are religious people in hospitals going along praying for people, but a doctor washing his hand before seeing his patients will do more for their survival rates than the prayers offered by their holy men. The evil God monster of Abraham is an all-powerful God and can do absolutely anything, except give any type of viable proof of his existence.

Often times, a theist will counter with the old, 'God works in mysterious ways', or stammer on about how God's not here for us to boss around and do our bidding in vain attempts to get him to prove himself to us, but in reality, it's just a bunch of crap. Studies have shown that when sick people are prayed for by fervent believers, they are more likely to be healed. Other, actual scientific studies, have shown that when you allow religious nutbags to carry out their own studies, they tend to be skewed towards their religious beliefs. I'm absolutely confident that a prayer method of healing can never stand up to the simple rigors of repeatability.

It is absolutely amazing the wealth of proof to disprove God you can come up with when turning a keen eye upon the absence of God's presence. The millions of children who starve to death, or who are beaten to death, or who are being raped throughout the world is each and every one a testament to the non-existence of a personal God. Especially if those children and/or their parents believe in one of the Abrahamic death cults.

And to counter with the idea that God is calling those children who die such horrible deaths home to heaven to be with him because he, for whatever reason, has suddenly decided heaven needs more children, is disgusting and vile. If your God is able to 'see all' and watches these children die slow agonizing deaths over months or years due to starvation, malnutrition, rape, and outright murder and do nothing, or to be able to watch children be repeatedly raped by gangs of men and not smite the men on the spot, then your God is either not real or quite malevolent. If you the reader were ever attacked by an adult as a child and an invisible hand didn't swoop in to protect you, then you know exactly what I mean. Many victims have often asked, 'Where was God when x happened to me?'

Even in the house of the lord, the travesties go unchallenged by God himself as the priests of the Catholic church molest countless young children right under the nose of the Almighty. How many of those innocent boys tell stories of God having any type of direct intervention to protect and defend them from the pedophile priests? None. In the Middle East, old men buy little girls as brides and take them home and rape them with all the sanctity of their faith, family, friends, and neighbors. Common practice. How many stories come out of the Middle East of Allah personally stepping in to help one of these children? None!

And why not? God steps in all the time to help people, doesn't he? You always hear these stories of people surviving horrible accidents with little or no injury and surely, logically, it must be divine intervention. Yes, of course, clearly you are special enough that the creator of everything in the entire universe has a personal interest in you. He is going to stop and take enough time out from watching small children starve to death to give a shit about whether you survive rolling your Lexus after drinking six or seven glasses of the Jesus juice at the church softball game. You hear more stories about Bigfoot or an alien spacecraft hovering over an airport than you do about God taking direct steps to intervene in anything. I can't honestly say I've ever heard of God actively stepping in to prevent a molestation, but you can bet if this book ever gets popular you'll start hearing such stories. That wacky human intellect...

The closest this all-powerful God can seem to come to manifesting himself in any corporeal way is burn the face of his rape victim, the Virgin Mary, into the occasional piece of toast. Oddly enough, he always requires the assistance of a toaster to get his message across and it's never even a very clear picture.

One would think the almighty could at least burn his images in 1080p high-resolution.

I've never seen someone pull a toasted piece of bread with Mary's face on it from a fresh, unmolested loaf, either. The first reaction of the believer to that last statement would almost certainly be, 'That's crazy. Burned toast without a toaster?' I say no, that's closing in on being a miracle in my book. Of course, due to the traditions of Islam and Catholicism, you may need you to define the term 'unmolested'.

But why stop there? If God is going to toss aside the mandate of faith and literally give you a sign of his existence, why stop there? Why stop with a grainy 640x480 resolution 'it might be, it might not be' the Virgin Mary or the image of her illegitimate rape baby, Jesus, when you could expound the knowledge of the universe? With the power of God, you could put an end to all religious war forever, even if you insisted on having burned bread as your main medium for communication. Imagine if every toaster the world over, without alteration by the hand of man, began to produce toast that read, 'The Coptic Jews are doing it right, so stop killing each other and quit being a dick in my name.'.

Some people are so indoctrinated, so infected in the mind that I doubt even this would sway them. There would be official fatwas against toasters. People who are caught owning toasters would be put to death and, of course, the Coptic Jews would have to be slaughtered whether they owned toasters or not.

I have to say at this point that if every toaster I encountered were to burn out a personal message from God to me and everyone else could see it, i.e. I'm not going insane, then that would certainly give me pause for consideration. As I sit here and evaluate my inner person, stirred by the very thought of such gripping proof, I've established that I truly do love toast especially with an unhealthy slab of butter and served with eggs and bacon. Mmm bacon. . . manna from heaven, if you'll pardon the expression. Therefore, I would at the very least have to acknowledge the existence of the toast God, but I still don't know if I'd kill in his name. Perhaps if more bacon were at stake. . . In the name of the bacon, the eggs, and the holy toast I pray.

Taa daaa!

Chapter 4. And God Made Woman

"An atheist believes that a hospital should be built instead of a church. An atheist believes that a deed must be done instead of a prayer said. An atheist strives for involvement in life and not escape into death. He wants disease conquered, poverty vanished, war eliminated." ~Madalyn Murray O'Hair

A picture of the prophet Mohammed, along with Buraq and Gabriel, visits Hell, and see a demon punishing "shameless women" who had exposed their hair to strangers. For this crime of inciting lust in men, the women are strung up by their hair.
Persian, 15th century

Women of the world hear me! You are disgusting and loathsome. Your beauty is nothing more than a trap to make men do vile things and take their eyes from the wonder of God. Your very nature brings out the worst in men; you are pathetic, you are unworthy, you are filth and scum. Your touch defiles me. Do you know how I know this? The bible tells me so.

"And the Lord spake unto Moses, saying, Speak unto the children of Israel, saying, If a woman have conceived seed, and born a man child: then she shall be unclean seven days; according to the days of the separation for her infirmity shall she be unclean. . . . But if she bears a maid child, then she shall be unclean two weeks . . ." Leviticus 12:1-5

"And I looked, and, lo, a Lamb stood on the mount Sion, and with him an hundred forty and four thousand, having his Father's name written in their foreheads. . . . And they sung as it were a new song before the throne, and before the four beasts, and the elders: and no man could learn that song but the hundred and forty and four thousand, which were redeemed from the earth. These are they which were not defiled with women; for they are virgins. These are they which follow the Lamb withersoever he goeth." Revelation 14:1-4

You are worth just over half what a man is worth. If you were bought and sold under the law of the Lord, your value would be less than that of a man. Why should you expect equal pay and fair treatment when you're little better than half a person?

"And the Lord spake unto Moses, saying, Speak unto the children of Israel, and say unto them, When a man shall make a singular vow, the persons shall be for the Lord by thy estimation. And

thy estimation shall be of the male from twenty years old even unto sixty years old, even thy estimation shall be fifty shekels of silver, after the shekel of the sanctuary. And if it be a female, then thy estimation shall be thirty shekels. And if it be from five years old even unto twenty years old, then thy estimation shall be of the male twenty shekels, and for the female ten shekels. And if it be from a month old even unto five years old, then thy estimation shall be of the male five shekels of silver, and for the female thy estimation shall be three shekels of silver. And if it be from sixty years old and above; if it be a male, then thy estimation shall be fifteen shekels, and for the female ten shekels."
Leviticus 27:1-7

There is the obvious argument that men are bigger and stronger and literally would have been more useful in the environment in which they lived. Hunting, sheep/cattle herding, murdering non-believers, all these things can be done better by men. Women are physically inferior, period! Feminists this is your chance to cast your stones. . . but you don't have any stones, so just shut up and keep reading.

And in Islam, you have half a brain...

"Call in two male witnesses from among you, but if two men cannot be found, then one man and two women whom you judge fit to act as witnesses.." *Quran Sura 2:282*

You often hear of the great men of the Bible, many of which had many wives and concubines. How many women heroes are there in the Bible? How many women heroes who have dozens of husbands and lovers? None, because men aren't 'things', but women are clearly the disposable property of men.

> *"But king Solomon loved many strange women, together with the daughter of Pharaoh, women of the Moabites, Ammonites, Edomites, Zidonians, and Hittites . . . And he had seven hundred wives, princesses, and three hundred concubines." I Kings 11:1-3*

You are wonderful, beautiful, intelligent creatures, and believe it or not, you do not deserve to be treated like shit. Does that thought surprise you? If you are a follower of any branch of the Abrahamic faith, you have been taught since childhood that you are not equal to a man. Not only are you enslaved to an evil, non-extant god, but you're also the servant of a flawed and insecure being called man, so sayeth the lord.

> *"Wives, submit yourselves unto your own husbands, as it is fit in the Lord." Colossians 3:18*

And on top of all that, you are the one who is to blame, not only when you do wrong, but for the wrong done by men. You are soooo sexy and men are such pigs that by merely seeing your hair a man will sin in his mind, thus damning his soul. And, since it was your slutty ways that caused him to sin, then you should suffer too. And that's just if he sins in his mind. What happens to her if he actually acts on his sinful thoughts? She dies by stoning.

> *"If any man take a wife, and go in unto her . . . and say, I took this woman, and when I came to her, I found her not a maid . . . and the tokens of virginity be not found for the damsel: Then they shall bring out the damsel to the door of her father's house, and the men of her city shall stone her with stones that she die . . ." Deuteronomy 22:13-21*

There are a couple of issues at play here. One is that although it sounds kind of bad, 'Oh goodness, she's not a virgin,' what is really being said is she had sex. Merely the act of parting her legs earns her a stoning, even if she was not complicit. The other issue is moving beyond the fact she's being punished at all for acting on a basic animalistic need, it has to do with the severity of the punishment. Stoning her? Really? To death? There are many places in the bible where a child is slain by their parents and one of the first things Christians want to do is distance themselves from it by pulling out the, 'That's the old covenant with God' crap. To them I say, Jesus said:

> *"Do not think that I have come to abolish the Law or the Prophets; I have not come to abolish them but to fulfill them." Matthew 5:17*

That's right. Keenly remember that Jesus was a Jew and believed in all the teachings of the Old Testament and to him women are property. His point was that the people were doing it wrong. Aww shucks. So now, most all the Christians live by the teachings of Christ, but ignore the Hebrew laws. You're not supposed to be a Christian. You're supposed to be a kind, loving, giving JEW and not turn your back on the Old Testament. The Old Testament, as previously discovered, believes women are worth half what a man is worth.

What does the bible say about male virgins? What if a woman marries a man and discovers he's not a virgin? The topic doesn't come up and it's not likely to, as men often possessed many wives and were presumed to have already had sex.

When I was going to elementary school as a boy, all of my teachers were women and I don't know of any who weren't Christian. How do you explain away the teachings of the apostle Paul who wrote to Timothy and said,

> *"Let the woman learn in silence with all subjection. But I suffer not a woman to teach, nor to usurp authority over the man, but to be in silence." I Timothy 2:11-15*

I think it's funny to listen to Muslim apologists talking about how far they've come in addressing the rights of women.

They talk about the progress they've made and how in some countries women can now drive or girls can now go to school without fear of attack from fanatics. These are the apologists speaking. They want you to ignore the truth. The very fact that now, in the second decade of the 21st century, they still have to apologize for things that are happening to women today, exposes the flaws in the system.

The list of Jewish crimes against women is clearly documented in the bible. If you go on the Old Testament, the Jews decided the evil God monster had given them the land of the Canaanites and they slaughtered anyone who got in their way to claim the land, already owned and live on by these other peoples. Killing every man, woman, or man child who lived in the cities who stood between them and where they thought there land was. The virgin girls were taken as sex slaves. Thankfully the Jews don't do that anymore.

The list of Christian crimes against women is as long as my arm. Although the Inquisition led by the Catholic Church during the 14th-18th centuries was intended to root out witchcraft, it is undeniable it was clearly used as a method of control and subjugation for women. The estimates of the numbers of women burned at the stake during the Inquisition ranges from the tens of thousands into the millions.

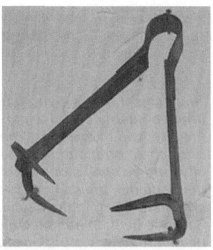

Breast ripper (15th century) at the torture museum in
Freiburg im Breisgau Photo by I. Stöcklin

Although Christianity and Judaism have put their more
barbaric practices against women behind them, Islam still needs
its apologists. But Islam and Christianity base their fundamental
core treatment and mentality toward women from Judaism, and
we all know what the Old Testament says about women. Islam,
never one to be outdone, makes sure a woman knows her place.

**"Men have authority over women
because God has made the one superior
to the other, and because they spend
their wealth to maintain them. Good
women are obedient. They guard their
unseen parts because God has guarded
them. As for those from whom you fear
disobedience, admonish them and
forsake them in beds apart, and beat
them." Sura 4:34**

Rape a married woman and what happens? You and your
victim are stoned to death. But why? Why are you the male
stoned to death? Well, because you have shamed another man.
By having sex with the man's wife/fiancée, he can no longer be
certain of the parentage of the children she bears. That other
man's family line has been tainted. And, of course, from now on

when the man has sex with his wife he fears she'll be secretly fantasizing about her rapist. She gets stoned to death essentially because she didn't scream loud enough to bring someone to her aid.

> *"If a damsel that is a virgin be betrothed unto an husband, and a man find her in the city, and lie with her; Then ye shall bring them both out unto the gate of the city, and ye shall stone them with stones that they die; the damsel, because she cried not, being in the city; and the man, because he hath humbled his neighbour's wife: so thou shalt put away evil from among you." Deuteronomy 22:23-24*

The idea of stoning a rape victim because she didn't cry out has so many flaws in and of itself it's pathetic. Just another testament that the Bible teaches us all women are whores. Surely it was her fault. What if the attacker snuck up on his victim and either covered her mouth or otherwise rendered her unable to call out? Well, the thinking is that she shouldn't have put herself in the position to get snuck up on, deserved to get raped, and has earned being stoned.

A man rapes an unmarried woman and what happens? He gives her father 50 shekels of silver and gets to marry her... but only if he's caught. If he doesn't get caught, he's officially off the hook and her precious hymen is gone, which is a potential death sentence for her considering the laws of their merciful God.

> *"If a man find a damsel that is a virgin, which is not betrothed, and lay hold on her, and lie with her, and they be found; Then the man that lay with her shall give unto the damsel's father fifty shekels of silver, and she shall be his wife; because he hath humbled her, he may not put her away all his days." Deuteronomy 22:28-29*

How many girls have been raped, lost their virginity, and then found themselves being stoned to death the day after their wedding? Imagine being a little girl and getting raped and then living with the sheer weight of dread and fear for years. Your wedding and funeral separated by the span of a few horrifying hours.

It's not uncommon or surprising to read in the news that some monk in Taiwan has set himself on fire as a form of protest. The self-immolation of a man in Tunisia set off protests and began what is known as the Arab Spring that spread like wildfire across the Middle East in early 2011.

Did you happen to know that little girls in the Middle East also have a tendency to set themselves on fire? They are so traumatized by the rape itself and in such fear that they'll die a slow, public, and painful death at the hands of the very people who are supposed to protect them, that they choose the agony of death by fire instead. These deaths tend to go unreported, hidden by the family members.

But wait a second... let's take a look at biblical examples of how a godly man protects his daughters:

> *"Before they had gone to bed, all the men from every part of the city of Sodom, both young and old, surrounded the house. They called to Lot, 'Where are the men who came to you tonight? Bring them out to us so that we can have sex with them.'*
>
> *Lot went outside to meet them and shut the door behind him and said, 'No, my friends. Don't do this wicked thing. Look, I have two daughters who have never slept with a man. Let me bring them out to you, and you can do what you like with them. But don't do anything to these men, for they have come under the protection of my roof.'"*
> *Genesis 9:4-8*

In this particular story, the girls were spared, but that's not really the point. And wait...who is Lot? Isn't Lot Abraham's nephew? He's the nephew of the father of the Abrahamic religion and a man so upstanding that angels were sent to save him from the destruction of Sodom, and he's trying to pitch his virgin daughters to a horny mob of men? In Lot's defense, the men he was protecting weren't ordinary men, they were angels... That makes it all ok. If two men who you knew in your heart to be angels, backed by the almighty power of God, showed up at your doorstep and a horde of horny homosexual Hebrews demanded to rape them, it's just natural to think to toss your virgin daughters out to be gang-raped rather than let the angels go out and open up a can of god sized whoop ass. Such a ridiculous moral example.

But really, there's a lot wrong with this story. Two angels make their way to Lot's place completely unmolested (there's that word again that may send priests and Muslim men running for a dictionary) and were so at ease in their surroundings that they originally wanted to spend the night in the city square. We see in the book of Judges that the purpose of stopping at the city square was the hope someone would see you there and offer you hospitality. But Lot convinces the angels to stay with him instead. They go in his house and visit for a while, then every single man both young and old from every quarter of the city showed up beating on the door wanting to have sex with the male angels. Really? Every man in the entire city? Yep, according to the holy and infallible word of God, every man young and old from every quarter of the city wanted to rape the angels. And all these rock hard horny men turned down the opportunity to have two young virgin girls and threatened to rape the elderly Lot instead? Really?

And it gets worse... How? Well, the angels save Lot and his family, not counting his wife of course because she's a filthy whore, and tell him to go to the mountains so they'll be safe. Lot, knowing better than the angels of the Lord, convinces them to let him go to another city called Moab rather than the mountains because he's too old and feeble to make such a trip. The angels conceded and yet where did Lot go? A cave in the. . .wait for it. . . mountains!

So, what happens in the cave? It's just old man Lot and his two virgin daughters. Being the whorish, filthy sluts they are, because they're female, the two daughters decide to get Lot drunk so they can have sex with him and bear children from him. The first night, the girls get Lot drunk on wine and the eldest daughter has sex with him. The second night, they did the same thing, but the younger daughter was the one doing papa. They got him so drunk that on both occasions, the Bible is keen to point out, Lot didn't remember anything of the events. But wait. . . you got an elderly man so drunk on wine that he couldn't remember anything and yet he was still able to get it up and actually. . . produce? Right. Twice? Uh-huh.

But you see here again how women are vilified in the bible? Whores! I'd almost bet there was no wine involved and Lot raped his own daughters, got them pregnant, and then blamed them. He may have been the one using wine to get the girls drunk so he could rape them.

> **"Consider the treatment of women. For millennia, the world's greatest prophets and theologians have applied their collective genius to the riddle of womanhood. The result has been polygamy, sati, honor killing, punitive rape, genital mutilation, forced marriages, a cultic obsession with virginity, compulsory veiling, the persecution of unwed mothers, and other forms of physical and psychological abuse so kaleidoscopic in variety as to scarcely admit of concise description." ~Sam Harris**

Funny thing is that a few chapters before when Abraham is talking with the Lord and with his wife Sarah, we learn that a person cannot conceive without the blessing of the Lord. Sarah was in her nineties and complaining that the Lord, whom her husband was apparently talking to in their living room, had not granted her a child. So the Lord tells her straight up that within a year she will be with child and the stupid bitch doesn't believe him. Women are so stupid. Then the Lord calls her on it after he's literally already read her mind, and she denies it and he pretty much calls her a liar. Stupid bitch. Just like all the rest.

Back to the girls. Not only did each girl conceive after only one, ummm sitting, with a drunk, elderly man, but they each bore a son who went on to be the father of an entire people. The eldest daughter bore Moab, father of the Moabites and the youngest bore Ben-Ammi, father of the sons of Ammon.

And the bible doesn't label what the girls do as bad. On the contrary, it even explains multiple times that the girls are doing it because they want to ensure the family line of Lot. The only indication the Bible gives of it being a shady deal is that the girls have to get their father drunk to do it. Again, the fact they bore fathers of nations would be considered proof of God's approval of their actions, or at least the author's approval of their actions.

But all this about how Lot tried to toss his daughters out to the wolves is an isolated incident, right? No. In fact, in the book of Judges it tells of a man referred to only as 'a Levite', from the remote hill country of Ephraim, who found himself a concubine in Bethlehem and he had a similar experience. Oddly enough, throughout the story, it refers to the woman as his wife and as his concubine. Either way, whether she was the same woman or not is irrelevant. On his way back home, the Levite passed several towns but refused to stay the night in them because they were not populated with Israelites. They finally make it to Gibeah, a good wholesome town full of Israelites (Benjamites to be specific), and make their way to the town square hoping someone will take them in for the night. The Levite laments that no one has stopped to offer them a place to rest, but he doesn't mention anything about ravenous hordes of horny homosexual Hebrews. Finally, a kind old man stops by and offers the Levite and his party, which consists of his concubine, a male servant and a couple of donkeys, a warm place to stay the night. He gives them food and feeds the donkeys for the Levite, a stranger he just met. Then suddenly, just like in Sodom, the hordes of horny homosexual Hebrews appears and wants to have sex with the Levite...

"While they were enjoying themselves, some of the wicked men of the city surrounded the house. Pounding on the door, they shouted to the old man who owned the house, "Bring out the man who came to your house so we can have sex with him." The owner of the house went outside and said to them, "No, my friends, don't be so vile. Since this man is my guest, don't do this outrageous thing. Look, here is my virgin daughter, and his concubine. I will bring them out to you now, and you can use them and do to them whatever you wish. But as for this man, don't do such an outrageous thing." But the men would not listen to him. So the man took his concubine and sent her outside to them, and they raped her and abused her throughout the night, and at dawn they let her go. At daybreak, the woman went back to the house where her master was staying, fell down at the door and lay there until daylight. When her master got up in the morning and opened the door of the house and stepped out to continue on his way, there lay his concubine, fallen in the doorway of the house, with her hands on the threshold. He said to her, "Get up; let's go." But there was no answer. Then the man put her on his donkey and set out for home." Judges 19:22-28

What an absolutely horrible story! And you realize the girls in this story are very likely to be under the age of twelve. A murderous group of men starts banging on your door and your first thought is to toss out your nine-year-old daughter? Again, a kind and godly person offers up his virgin daughter to fend off a horde of God's chosen people who've gone mad with geriatric homosexual lust, to save a person he just met. And again, it would seem raging hordes of horny Hebrew men are impervious to the wiles of little girls and turned away the offer of a female virgin and the Levite's concubine. Since the Levite had just taken the concubine as his wife, it's safe to presume she too was a young girl, just not a virgin thanks to Mr. Levite. The point, in fact, she was unwilling to be his bride and after four months returned home to her parents in Bethlehem. He had gone back and gotten her and they were returning to his home city when this tragedy happened. But again the recurring motif here is that when in danger, sacrifice the women first.

This story differs from the one about Lot because even though the horde apparently refused the virgin and the concubine, the Levite sent his new bride out anyway. And then he apparently went to bed. All that walking through the desert and tossing the pre-pubescent girl he loved, or at least the pre-pubescent girl he just bought, out to her rape and demise takes a toll on a person. No further thought of her from him till he trips over her on his way leaving town. If you keep reading the story you learn it's good he got a solid night's rest. He was so insulted because the hordes of horny homosexual Hebrews had tried to rape him and killed his concubine that he personally cut up her body and sent the parts of her to every tribe of Israel.

Why do you suppose it was that these men had no want for a virgin female? Perhaps these young girls were particularly homely? No, I suspect the reason was that the Israelites were allowed to keep virgin females for themselves as the spoils of war. Virgin girls were old hat to them; a disposable commodity, especially in times of war. I suspect the reason the concubine was sent out and not the virgin was because between the two of them, the concubine, with her lack of an intact hymen, was the one with the least value.

And what happens to you when you die, ladies? What evidence in the bible does it give you that women will find equal treatment in the afterlife? Women are given object/slave status throughout the bible. Women are almost always portrayed as wicked. Many of the great men of the bible who fell from grace did so because of the influence of a woman. What makes you think you're going to even be allowed in the presence of God?

The 144,000 who are called to sing the song of God are called in part because they have not been 'defiled' with women.

How many female disciples were there? Hmmm. In John 6:44 after Jesus uses five loaves of bread and two fish and feeds a multitude of people, how many people did he feed? It says he fed five thousand MEN. Now, some will argue this was even more of a miracle because they didn't count the women back then, therefore he may have fed closer to ten thousand people, but did you notice that little phrase, 'they didn't count the women'?

No, Christian ladies, have no fear and continue to pray to your God, Jesus, and when you make it to heaven you'll find you have a new body and are reborn. Yes, you'll be a virgin again, with the all so precious hymen intact. At least, now you know where all those virgins come from that God gives to the Muslim suicide bombers. Good luck with that.

Even if the evil God monster of the Abrahamic religions does exist, how could you possibly want to follow HIM?

Chapter 5. It's a Miracle?

"If every trace of any single religion were wiped out and nothing were passed on, it would never be created exactly that way again. There might be some other nonsense in its place, but not that exact nonsense. If all of science were wiped out, it would still be true and someone would find a way to figure it all out again." ~Penn Jillette

Penn & Teller
Image courtesy of Destination360

The Merriam-Webster online dictionary defines a miracle as, "An extraordinary event manifesting divine intervention in human affairs". Many Christians use the miracles of Christ as the bedrock for their belief systems, but upon closer inspection, one can apply the simplest of explanations to rule out any form of true divine intervention. And even worse, some of his miracles are mentioned in more than one book of the Bible, presumably by different authors, and the two stories don't match up. The miracles of the other 'prophets' are just as numerous and bear just as much substance. They're all miracles. . . if you ask the guy telling the story.

I saw a stage act in Vegas. . . well, ok, I didn't actually see the act, but I watched their show on Showtime and it . . . ok fine, I didn't watch their show on Showtime, but I did see it on YouTube. . . Sigh, so, when trolling Facebook, if one of my friends posted a clip of Penn and Teller's work, I would watch (most of) the clip and let me tell you these guys are awesome! There's this little guy, he is absolutely hilarious and then there's the other guy who talks a lot and he's ok too. Anyway, the point to all this is I've seen better miracles on a Vegas stage than are listed for Jesus. The little guy can make rabbits come out of his hat and the big guy. . . well, he pretty much just talks a lot, but a rabbit from an empty hat sounds like some fairly miraculous stuff to me.

And, here's the real clincher, I just happened to see it with my very own eyes. No one told me he did it. I didn't read it in a book. With my baby greens, I saw a video recording of a man pulling a rabbit out of a hat from various camera angles. Do I believe he really pulled a real rabbit from that hat, which I saw and believed to be empty? Hell yeah, I do! I saw it with my own eyes!

But wait... what if I didn't see it with my own eyes? What if someone told me they saw it? Should I believe them and believe you can really pull rabbits out of empty hats? Ok, let's go one step further. Let's say this guy tells me his grandfather fifty years ago saw a man pull not one rabbit out of an empty hat, but several thousand. Enough to feed five thousand men. The story is even more grandiose now so surely that must make it even more true, right? Ok, last step. Let's imagine that guy whose grandfather told him such a wonderful and true (because grandpa says so) story writes this drivel down, convinces his friends, and starts spreading it around. Then someone stuffs away a copy in a cave and two thousand years later someone digs it up. Does that make it even more true? Did the little guy really pull a live rabbit out of an empty hat? Is it a magic trick gone extremely right or clear proof of divine intervention?

Imagine if these two magically inclined comedians, or comedy inclined magicians, however you like it, were somehow thrust back in time a couple of thousand years and had a mindset bent on mischief... Who knows? We might even have a holiday with an invisible rabbit showing up out of nowhere and leaving candy for all the little boys and girls. Well, not girls. They're unclean.

So, back to our prophets, the little guy goes into town first and spends a couple of days playing the blind beggar. The big guy goes along telling people how awesome he is, doing some fancy magic tricks and telling them how they need to follow him. He takes his followers into town and when they need a really big miracle, he happens along the little guy and heals his blindness. Now the followers are drooling with fervency. These two con men skip along from town to town until tragedy strikes. Things get out of hand and the big guy ends up on the cross. Damn! What's the little guy to do? He decides to keep the game rolling, of course. A man's gotta eat! He sneaks the body out of the tomb, claims the tall man's divinity, opens a church, and starts raking in the dough, or sheep, as it were. After decades of loyal followers relaying simple magic tricks as miracles and blowing them out of proportion to further their own claims and beliefs, you have the beginning of a religion. The disappearing thumb trick evolves into the story of how the big guy removed his own arm to prove his divinity, etc.

The disappearing thumb trick
Image courtesy of hubpages.com

Often, theists will use ancient historians to try to prove the existence of Jesus. Ok, fine. I'll concede it is possible Jesus was a real person. However, none of the historians they cite actually lived at the time of Jesus. Most of them weren't even born until 30-200 years after Jesus died. And although these historians do speak of Christians and of the execution of Christ, a story propagated by Christians, that mere fact alone does not grant him Godhood, nor does it prove the existence of God or Jesus. All it proves is that there were Christians around causing trouble and claiming they followed a man named Christ who they claim was executed by the Romans at the behest of the Jews. It should be noted that despite being meticulous record keepers, the Romans made no note of these events and none of the secular accounts mention anything about miracles performed by Jesus. One would think there would be all manner of secular writings considering in the book of John it reads:

> **"Jesus did many other things as well. If every one of them were written down, I suppose that even the whole world would not have room for the books that would be written." John 21:25**

Yet we have nothing. Zilch, zero, squat! But of course, John would make this claim.

David Koresh mug shot photo

I can find historical documents that prove the existence of David Koresh and that he had a large group of followers who believed he could perform miracles. In fact, a brief internet search will show that decades after his death there are still people out there called Koreshians who believe he is the Messiah. However, simply stating something doesn't make it true and if David Koresh were truly God, it would have been a perfect opportunity for him to walk out through the flames unharmed on national television and quash all doubts. Did it happen? Nope. Dead as a doornail. So do you think in a thousand years we'll have Koreshians blowing themselves up in malls? Why not?

Joseph Smith Jr

Joseph Smith Jr of Mormon fame was shot in a jail cell, tried to jump out the window to escape and died in the fall. Dozens of people there and no one sees anything supernatural. A single 'believer' onsite claims after the fact to have seen Smith be resurrected or some crap. Given a hundred years for his followers to spread his nonsensical word and now millions believe he sits at the left hand of God. He and Jesus hanging out up there with God, watching little kids starve. Hell, the guy couldn't even take a couple of bullets and a twenty-foot drop to the ground, so I'm hard pressed to believe he's any type of Messiah. Neo from the Matrix could use his mind to stop bullets and could fly. Joseph Smith Jr performed a similar 'miracle', except he used his internal organs to stop the bullets and his flying skills were somewhat lacking.

Muhammad was a real work of art. He performed more miracles than you can shake a stick at. After fifteen to sixteen hundred years, his followers have spread into the billions and the tales of his miracles are great. Split the moon into two pieces and put it back together, or so his followers claim. In fifteen hundred years, the Koreshians will probably believe their messiah healed the blind and did all kinds of things his followers of today will make up to try to convince themselves and their children of his divinity. Then the children will tell the stories to their children adding even more grandiose coloring to the lies and then those children, none of whom were actually alive at the time, will write down the books of Koresh and before long they will have themselves a bible and a messiah worth killing for.

And they are always, 'coming back'. With the exception of Muhammad who even his followers believe him to be dead and never to return, most of these so-called seers claim they are coming back. Joseph Smith Jr will someday return. Jesus will someday return. David Koresh will someday return. Blah blah blah. Return now! Brother, it's been two thousand years since Jesus died. . . dude ain't coming back!

The miracle of Jesus rising from the dead was fake, a hoax. His followers pulled his body from his grave and then they gave him a proper burial, no doubt. It was a follower who claimed the body of Jesus from Pontius Pilate and allegedly offered up his own tomb for Jesus to be buried in. There's no guarantee his body ever got there, beyond the claim of the hoaxers. Then they propagated the lie of Jesus' resurrection, complete with a tale of men shining like lightning outside his tomb telling passersby he had risen from the grave. Well, it depends on which story you read. Some claim Mary and/or Mary Magdalene found the empty tomb.

Why would his followers do such a thing? First of all, to avoid the shame of being wrong, especially if they had claimed all along he would be resurrected. I suspect Jesus and his followers probably didn't make such a claim and it was added later. I say this primarily because if such claims had been made, I think it extremely unlikely the Romans or Hebrews would have left the tomb unattended. After all the commotion, I would imagine quite a few interested parties would have stuck around to see if he would fulfill the prophecy. One would think the Jews would be extremely keen to learn if they had just crucified their would-be messiah, and Pontius Pilate would be very interested to discover if his old Pagan gods were real or if the God of the Jews was real.

Secondly, for the same reason the Romans and Jews would have stuck around and watched for his resurrection, his followers would have wanted to further the idea of Jesus fulfilling prophecy and his brand of Judaism (we now call it Christianity) becoming dominant. And lastly, because people seldom give up power and control once they have it. In reality, I suspect the greatest hoax of all time was probably pulled off by a very few people when they convinced the rest of Jesus' followers that he'd been resurrected. Perhaps the twelve disciples are actually the twelve deceivers or the twelve dupes. He didn't even look like himself. So much so that he had to convince some of his followers it was really him. Some Christians I've spoken with attribute this change in appearance to the effects of being resurrected but there are many people resurrected throughout the bible and not a single other seems to have an identity crisis and everyone knows who they are. The only person resurrected in the Bible who didn't look the same way post-resurrectus was Christ. And these aren't secular claims made by people trying to disprove the divinity of Jesus, these are his own follower's words written in his own bible.

If Jesus survived the actual crucifixion, with the help of a Roman soldier working on the inside and Joseph of Arimathea whisking him away to safety, he would surely have been badly swollen and bruised from the event. This would explain why people would have had a difficult time recognizing him. The problem with this is that it removes divinity and we're left with the atheist mandate that there is no God. If he had been resurrected with the glory and power of almighty God, he should have been healed from head to toe and easily recognizable. Properly paid off Roman soldiers could have placed the spikes just under his hands and feet rather than through them so he could grab onto and stand upon them, and the final death blow by the Roman spear actually being a mere cut on the side to speed the end of the charade. However, the sleight of hand tricks with the spikes during crucifixion is one thing, but the very public lashing he took at the hands of the Romans would have been something he probably couldn't have faked. I would think if he survived the crucifixion the only reason he stayed around for such a short time afterward was that he caught an infection or otherwise succumbed to the wounds sustained during the beatings. A story ending with him rising up into heaven to meet God is so much better than him getting gangrene in his legs and dying a slow and horrible death. If he was the real Messiah, he should have publicly risen up from the dead and united all of Israel under his rule and protection and should have cast out the invading Romans. Did that happen? No. It's no wonder the Jews don't consider him the true Messiah. If you do all the frilly stuff on the side that point to you as being the chosen one, but you don't actually do what the Messiah was supposed to do, then what good are you? Oh, well, the claim is made that although he didn't unite the tribes of Israel in life he's going to do it in the afterlife and therefore fulfill the prophecy. Sounds to me like people making stuff up as they go along.

> **"When I was 14 a chaplain at school gave me a reading list. I read everything and I went back to him with a question: How can you really believe in this stuff?"**
> **~A.C. Grayling**

If someone played his part in his stead after his death and burial, it's not a farfetched idea that this could be the reason his followers had a hard time recognizing him. One of the followers may have stepped in as a replacement. It would not surprise me to learn of the accounts of his appearance being outright fabrications as the people he was 'appearing' to were his loyal followers, i.e. fellow hoaxers.

Here's something else to consider. In the book of Mark it tells of Jesus' arrest at Gethsemane and in this tale, it says on the night before he was arrested Jesus stepped away from the main party to 'pray' while three disciples, Peter, James, and John, all sat watch. Jesus is such an awe-inspiring Messiah these guys can't even stay awake long enough for him to pray.

Three times he steps away to pray and three times he comes back and they are all sleeping and he, the almighty son of God, chastises them and yet each time he returns they are asleep. I propose they had no idea Jesus was going to be arrested that night and any claim of such was added after the fact. There are some who believe Jesus was up on Gethsemane enjoying the pleasures of a young male disciple when the soldiers came.

> *"A young man, wearing nothing but a linen garment, was following Jesus. When they seized him, he fled naked, leaving his garment behind." Mark 14:51-52*

'Was following Jesus,' who had just come alone from the garden at Gethsemane where he was 'praying'. The assertion that Jesus was having gay sex the night most believers think he was pleading with God not to put him through the crucifixion will probably not sit well with many, but it makes more logical sense that he was out there getting his gay play on, rather than he is the risen God and was having a heart to heart with his almighty self. I don't know how true it is, but it makes you wonder two things. One is, why would a mostly naked young man be following Jesus around in the dark? And the other is... why would the author of Mark bother to mention it? I would be more likely to believe Judas intentionally identified the wrong person to the Roman soldiers and the person slipping away in his underwear was, in fact, Jesus.

There was a reason groups like the Council of Nicea decided to remove certain books from the main canon of the bible. Perhaps there's a little less 'miracle' and a lot more 'pay no attention to the man behind the curtain' going on than you've been led to believe.

Wouldn't want the Tin Man to find his brain now, would we?

Chapter 6. The Adversary

"But who prays for Satan? Who, in eighteen centuries, has had the common humanity to pray for the one sinner that needed it most?" ~Mark Twain

Mark Twain in the lab of Nikola Tesla, spring of 1894

Okay so who is the devil, Satan, and/or Lucifer? There is a whole slew of different versions or identities associated with that person who reigns in Hell, but most westerners think of Satan as the fallen angel Lucifer. Actually, the term Satan in ancient Hebrew means 'the adversary', so in that context it's not an individual's name but rather a description or title. In fact, the ancient Hebrew writings made no mention of the adversary being a 'fallen' angel at all. He was more like a prosecuting attorney for your soul. He and Jesus vie for souls before the eyes of God and when the day was over they'd drop off their paperwork to the multi-eyed beasties surrounding God's throne and head to the bar to knock back a couple of beers together.

It was the twisted minds of early Christianity who turned Lucifer into the beast he's become. Their efforts not only turned an otherwise angelic and beautiful creature into a disfigured demonic monster, but it also helped to undermine the competition. In an attempt to vilify the very popular Pagan god

Pan the early Christians usurped his image and applied a horrid, bastardized version to Lucifer. It's funny how not only did they cast him down, but at the same time they elevated him to Godhood. He can be anywhere at any time and can see anything and can get in your mind and knows all your darkest secrets and can make you do things…etc.

If there was war in heaven before man, which was followed by God's wars of man in the Old Testament, and followed by all the religion based wars since, and then according to the book of Revelation years and years of hell on Earth as God destroys all the nonbelievers, how can you even remotely, laughingly consider him a God of peace? Ok, so, Jesus talked some peace, but he also said he wasn't there to take away the old laws. He said he was not here to make peace, but to make war. And his followers have spilled blood in his name for two millennia. The God of the Jews was a horrible, murderous monster, based solely on his own books, and yet someone who would stand up against him is considered wicked and evil?

Archangel Michael Hurls the Rebellious Angels
into the Abyss Luca Giordano (1632-1705)

The God creature reads a lot like Megatron from the
Transformers series. 'Worship me and be my slave or perish!'
His loyal follower Starscream seems to worship his every step
and yet, no matter how hard Starscream tries and sacrifices to
please his master, his reward is a violent admonishment almost
always including the words, 'You have failed me yet again,
Starscream!'

So, about twenty-five hundred years ago, lord Megatron
stopped by and slaughtered a couple of million humans,
banished Optimus Prime and the Autobots back to Cybertron,
and then he forced some humans to write him up in a book as
God. He also ordered that in his book Optimus be described as
wicked and the purveyor of sin. After all this, he left. Then five
hundred years later, he sent Starscream back to Earth to make
sure we were still in check. Starscream noticed the people had
taken Megatron's book so literally they were killing each other off
in the form of burnt sacrifices. The people were not growing
enough to be the slave labor force lord Megatron wanted waiting
for him upon his return, so Starscream took it upon himself to

alter some of the rules. He talked about how wonderful it is in Cybertron and how when we die we'll all get to live there. Remember in the Old Testament of the mega-bible there's no mention of a Cybertron or that human souls will ever get there.

Some of the people actually started to worship Starscream and we all know how he is. Although he is a loyal follower of Megatron, he has an ambitious streak of his own and didn't see any harm in muddying the message a bit. He hinted that he and the almighty Megatron might be the same person. Now we're worshiping them both as Megatron and the only way we can get to Cybertron is by believing in Starscream and that he was our savior. Saving us from what, exactly? The wrath of the evil lord Megatron when he returns, of course.

Starscream sent word to Cybertron informing Megatron of what he had done and what do you think Megatron did? He smacked Starscream around, 'Once again you disappoint me, Starscream' and called him back to Cybertron. Then Megatron sent Soundwave back to undo the soft and cuddly image Starscream had left with the people. Soundwave made it clear there was only one Megatron and Soundwave was his prophet and this cult should worship with ultimate devotion. Non-believers were to be put to death or converted. Only then, once the mission of murder and conversion was complete would there be peace on Earth. His hatred for mankind compelled him to lay out rules making life absolutely miserable. Pray to Lord Megatron five times a day, enslave your women and cover them from head to toe, sacrifice the pleasures and teaching of this world for the mental slavery offered in the next, etc., so when lord Megatron returns they will be fervent, broken, unquestioning slaves ready to die for him.

So how does this not fit? I've taken a horrible sci-fi dictator and his sidekicks and dropped them in the place of God, Jesus, and Muhammad and no other alteration is needed. It requires no real stretch of the imagination to put any ego-maniacal villain with delusions of godhood in the place of God and the prophets of the Abrahamic religions. When lord Megatron returns he will unleash the armies of Cybertron upon the Earth and torture and murder those who do not worship him and enslave those who do.

It's so obvious from the writing of his own followers that if he actually exists God is a horrible monster and Jesus is little more than an apologist for this monster. So would someone who opposes these entities be considered a bad person or evil? Well, yes, based on the books written by the followers of Megatron. However, comparing our own sense of morality to that taught in the mega-bible, it could easily be argued that Optimus was actually a good guy. He became sick of watching how horrible Megatron treated those who worshipped and believed in him and decided a revolution was in order. Evidently, there were many who agreed with him because according to Megatron's own book a third of Cybertron joined the Autobots and rebelled. We know dictators often lie and skew the numbers in their favor, so I'm betting it was more like half of Cybertron who rebelled. Evidently, the evil God monster won and despite all his blatant malevolence, his followers keep wrapping it up as a message of peace and it continues to spread like a sugar coated plague.

Here's another question I've recently been entertaining intellectually... If God is an omnipresent, omnipotent creature who knows all and sees all AND if Lucifer and his minions were angels without the free will to question God, how could they revolt? What would make a mere angel think he could dethrone a being he knows in his heart cannot be dethroned? Ok fine, a deranged angel. Broken, perhaps defective, but seriously... I was raised to believe God knew my every thought and could watch every aspect of my life and still watch every petal on every flower on Earth. If this is the case, then only madness can explain why an angel in heaven would possibly imagine he could supplant such a being. And it's one thing to have such imaginings rattling around in your head, but a completely different thing to actually act on those thoughts. Somehow, a creature made perfect by a perfect God, has psychological issues and decides he wants to take over the throne of heaven. But then it must be taken a massive step further. This isn't just one angel, it's a third of the host of heaven who rebelled against God. I sat about wondering how a lowly angel could possibly get a full third of the host of heaven to follow him against a God they knew to be real. No faith crap, they knew, so how did he get them to turn from God? As this question gnawed at my mind, I decided I would step away from the keyboard and take in some news. Update my Facebook and whatnot. Then it dawned on me! Eureka, I said to myself! There was only one way Lucifer could spread the word of ungodliness so quickly and to so many.... Carrier Pigeons! Little messages of doom and despair tied to their little legs and sent out to the masses of heaven. Message reads: 'Turn away from the God you know and love, get turned into hideous monster creatures, and spend eternity in a lake of fire with me. 5pm Don't be late! Signed, Luci.'

Illustration for John Milton's "Paradise Lost"
by Gustave Doré, 1866

Ridiculous, right? Well, if I were writing this in the 1800s it might not seem so ridiculous. Fine, let's move heaven into the 21st century. Ok, we've all just suddenly realized that before mankind and before the war of the angels, they simply must have had a major news media outlet, the Yahweh Is King and Eternal Savior – YIKES - News Network (YNN), and OnYourFacebook in heaven. Who'd a thunk it? I suspect Lucifer's revolt was quite an easy sell. Angels all over heaven either in prostration to God, murdering some heavenly creature in God's name, or watching the slaying of those creatures in God's name on YNN, when suddenly they get an OYFacebook status update on their Gphone. 'Yahweh is bad, Lucifer is good. Like this post to vote for our guy Luci, ignore this post to vote for the other guy, lest he smite you.'

Although the book of Genesis never calls the serpent by any name, it is often presumed to be Lucifer. If you invoke the ancient Hebrew definition of Satan meaning 'the adversary', rather than a proper name, then by definition it could be equally argued that the serpent was Lucifer or was simply another entity in opposition to god. Essentially, god wanted humans to be ignorant slaves and the serpent, whomever it was, set them free.

In the book of Job, when Satan appears before God, it's actually God who incites the wager by being boastful and proud of Job for being such a godly man. Satan simply made the point that perhaps the reason Job was so godly was because God had blessed him and given him so much, and that if it were taken away Job would curse God. Rather than debating the matter, God simply says let's destroy all his stuff, don't harm his body, and see if you're right. So they destroy everything Job has, yet he passes this test and refuses to curse God. Then they meet again and again God is boastful and proudb and he adds the rub that Job has passed the test. Satan's response is that they've taken away all Lot's family and possessions, but he still has his health, so God lets Satan put boils on Lot and harm his body. Even though Job's wife tries to get him to curse God, another example of how you can point out a villain in the bible because they have vaginas, he once again passes the test.

But this time he passes with the help of several friends who stopped by and keep telling him how wonderful God is. He starts cursing the day he was born and goes on at length about suffering and misery, etc and I believe he would have cursed God had he been left alone, but his friends give him moral support, sort of.

One of the points I'm trying to make about Satan is that God is a vicious monster and Satan or 'the adversary' is actually on our side against this monster. Job says at one point that God is mean and vicious and. . . well, let's just hear it in Job's own words...

> *"He destroys both the blameless and the wicked. When a scourge brings sudden death, he mocks the despair of the*

> *innocent. When a land falls into the*
> *hands of the wicked, he blindfolds its*
> *judges." Job 9:22-23*

God is so mean and cruel that Job is cursing his life and even goes so far as to say that were he not so afraid of God, he would speak up.

> *"He is not a mere mortal like me that I*
> *might answer him, that we might*
> *confront each other in court. If only*
> *there were someone to mediate between*
> *us, someone to bring us together,*
> *someone to remove God's rod from me*
> *so that his terror would frighten me no*
> *more. Then I would speak up without*
> *fear of him, but as it now stands with*
> *me, I cannot." Job 9:32-35*

In the story, Job maintains he's blameless and wants to talk to God himself to argue his case. He wants God to tell him what sin he has committed and either be damned (die) for it or allowed to repent. His friends maintain that God is great and even rebuke Job for his continued proclamation of blamelessness, clearly stating that if he were really blameless, these things wouldn't be happening to him. Of course, he gets angry and snaps back at them. We in our everyday lives have tried to console a friend who is going through hard times and have had that friend lash out at us, so this part of the tale is not unusual. But based on the logic they all employ, i.e., 'I am blameless therefore God shouldn't be doing this to me' and 'If you were blameless this wouldn't be happening' they are all indeed correct. The one player who is not playing the game by the rules is God.

In the end, even God lashes out at the friends. Not for meddling in the wager between him and Satan, but rather for the same offenses Job was angry with them for. It would have been a completely different story if Satan had appeared to Job instead and told him if he cursed God he would be freed of the plagues and the fear of God. And I have no doubt that had Job been given the choice, he would rather have died an atheist death than to continue as a slave of God. Job did not swear against God directly only out of fear, sheer terror, nothing else.

I bet Satan, in this particular story, was quite frustrated indeed. Not only did three minions of God show up and minister to Job, essentially unbalancing the wager, but in the end Satan's overall point was right, but Job is so terrified shit-less of this monstrous God that the man can't bring himself to curse it. His fear of God is too great, not his love of God. You'll notice there's no mention of love or affection for God. It's all about fear and terror. Satan shouldn't have said Job was loyal to God because God blessed everything Job did and had. He should have said Job was loyal because he was scared out of his mind of the loving merciful God. If Satan would have appeared and simply been able to lift Job's fear of God, Job would have cursed God and never burned an animal in sacrifice again.

Now, you might argue the friends were not helping him because they did indeed indicate his sins must have been great to make God rebuke him, but really the overall theme of the entire conversation between them is how great God is. 'God is mighty this, God is mighty that, I am blameless, yet I wish I were dead and his rod removed from me.' 'God is mighty this, God is mighty that, if you were blameless his rod wouldn't be on you. Quit crying like a whiney baby.'

So I think the next time you're reading your bible and you see Satan or Lucifer or the Devil doing something wicked stop and look at the context of what's happening.

He might not be such a bad guy after all.

Chapter 7. Islam Means Peace?

"Asked whether suicide bombing can be justified as a measure to defend Islam, 26 percent of American Muslims age eighteen to twenty-nine said yes. That is one quarter of the adult American Muslims under the age of thirty, and no matter how you count the number of Muslims in America (estimates vary from 2 million to 8 million), that is a lot of people." ~Ayaan Hirsi Ali

Ayaan Hirsi Ali
Image Public Domain

Islam is a religion of peace and you're willing to kill me to prove it. It would hardly seem anyone in their right mind could even laughingly call Islam a religion of peace. Islam is the third, and worst, plague to be wrought on humanity. It is in fact only a cult of peace if everyone who doesn't believe is killed or converted. The standardization of the Islamic religion throughout all the world's worshippers would be the only way, but it's not that easy. The main schism in Islam has to do with whether the descendants of Muhammad should lead the faith or if just anyone can become a religious leader. That, of course, is a simplistic view, but in reality that is the difference. The Shi'ites believe in order to be a leader of Islam you must be a direct descendant of Muhammad, the Sunnis disagree and the two groups have been murdering each other from day one. Even though there are specific rules having to do with it being ok to lie and murder infidels but not fellow Muslims, they still found a way. All it took was the splitting of hairs about what makes a person a true Muslim before the blood began to flow. Now, just like with Christianity, there are thousands of little factions with their own leaders and their own interpretation of the blood-soaked merciful word of Allah.

With Christianity, there were lots of different factions in the beginning, but many of them were eventually unified together by the Roman Catholic Church. They held it together for centuries until King Henry of England, wanting a divorce, got tired of being bossed around by the pope and created the Church of England. Then the Protestants broke away and it was all downhill from there for the church. The pesky demons of science snuck in while the deacons were fighting amongst themselves and they shone the light of knowledge upon mankind. The damage to religion's ridiculous house of cards cannot be undone, but it will probably take another thousand years before we can remove this particularly pernicious form of infestation from the earth.

Something to consider is when a Muslim takes a life in the name of Allah, they can't be truly certain Allah really wanted that person dead at that time. You could argue that if Allah didn't want him dead then he wouldn't be dead, but by doing so you eliminate your argument of free will, which means the murderer actually had no choice in the matter. If that's the case, then everything that happens is God's will and there is no sin by man. All the Christians/Muslims murdered by non-believers were done so because God wanted them dead. But if, as most theists assert, there is a God and he gave us free will, then murdering someone in the name of Allah takes away Allah's chances down the road to bring that man to his light.

Imagine killing a man who would have, unbeknownst to anyone, converted to your brand of crazy anyway in a couple of years and made his way into heaven. Not only did you take his life, but you also took away his afterlife. You should burn in hell for that. We should go 'Old Testament' on your ass and make your next seven generations also burn in hell, regardless of the piety of their lives.

If heaven and hell are running a wager and the one with the most souls at the end of the day wins, then you are doing the work of the devil! By murdering people, whom you know to be infidels and sending them to hell before God can finish doing his works in their lives, then you are working against heaven. You are sending them to hell before he can bring them to his fold and, subsequently, you too should burn in hell.

> **The deeper study of the Koran, Hadith, and Arab history led me to believe that Islam had been cleverly devised on the principle of divide and rule. And its purpose is to enable the Arabs to dominate the rest of the world. I have no doubt the Prophet wanted to raise himself to the same status as Allah. Muhammad loved Arabia & its culture, and his one desire was to create a strong, conquering Arab nation that believed in him and propagated his name. This could only be achieved by imperial dominance." ~Anwar Shaikh**

Should Islam, as a religion, be feared? Hell yes! When Mohammed first started Islam, he lived in Mecca and had few followers. He was surrounded by Jews, Christians, and various tribes of pagans and infidels. By pagans, I'm referring to the Christian term meaning any person who worships a god/gods other than the God associated with the Jewish/Christian/Islamic faiths. 'Infidels' is an Islamic term for anyone who doesn't follow Islam. Being surrounded by hostile or potentially hostile peoples/religions, and with very few followers, Muhammad began preaching a message of peace and tolerance.

The peoples of these various religions reacted like most people do when someone new arrives on their doorstep preaching that their God is inferior and that they should change their ways. They became intolerant and eventually drove Mohammed and his followers out of Mecca. Which, to me, is somewhat ironic since Muhammad is supposed to be so close to Allah you'd think he and his followers would be impervious to such actions.

In any case, the newly formed religion of Islam relocated to the city of Medina, then known as the city of Yathrib, and Mohammed was able to unite the warring tribes of Medina under Islam. His base of followers reached a saturation point in the population where they outnumbered anyone who was not of Islam. As time went on and his list of followers grew, the message turned from that of peace to one of intolerance and, by the end of his life, to a message of hatred and outright murder. It's no surprise that there were those in Medina who did not follow the teachings of Mohammed and equally no surprise in the knowledge that they were either assassinated or forcibly converted. 'Convert or Die' I believe is the proper term.

> **"Men never commit evil so fully and joyfully as when they do it for religious convictions." ~Blaise Pascal**

Once Medina was securely under Mohammed's control, he turned his eye on Mecca and spent the next eight years warring with the tribes of Mecca until he and his followers finally conquered the city. Historical records vary as to why he warred with Mecca; did Mohammed start the conflict or were the followers of Islam provoked by raids and attacks by the tribes of Mecca? That's a tough call and I'll leave it to the historians to argue over, but I have a couple of thoughts on the issue.

Firstly, throughout history, religions have murdered and oppressed those who believed in something other than the main doctrine, so it's no wonder the peoples of Mecca would resist the teachings of Mohammed. He was basically saying, 'Your religion is wrong and your prophets are wrong or outdated. Here is a newer, stricter religion that promises to oppress you even more than your old religion.' I'm paraphrasing here. As a comedian and satirical author, I'm allowed a certain leeway. I'm almost certain this line of thinking in the minds of the people of Mecca played at least some role in the 'why' concerning the attacks on Mohammed and his followers.

Secondly, (I love the symmetry in this) throughout history religions have murdered and oppressed those who believed in something other than the main doctrine, so it's no wonder the peoples of Medina would move to forcibly convert and attack the city of Mecca, regardless of whether they were provoked or not. Basically saying, 'Your religion is wrong, etc. . . CONVERT OR DIE!'

So what does any of this have to do with the more modern question of whether or not we should fear, or at the very least be truly concerned about, the spread of Islam? Well, here again, we have a two-part answer:

First, in Islam if something is taught in the beginning (chronologically as it was written) of the Quran, then a new contradictory rule is taught near the end, it's the rule at the end that is to be followed. For example: If in the beginning, the Quran said everyone should wear red hats, then red hats are the only hats allowed. But near the end, it said Mohammed declared blue hats were the best and only blue hats should be worn. Then, according to Islam, henceforth the red hat rule is out and only blue hats should be worn. Well, the early teachings of Islam were of peace, but as time went on the message turned to intolerance and violence. This means the people we consider 'violent extremist' are actually following the Quran as it was meant to be followed. The 'peaceful' Muslims are basically dropping the ball when it comes to following the word of their religion. Let us all pray, well, not atheist like me, but the rest of you can go ahead, that the mass majority of Islam never figures this out.

Second, Islam is moving across the world at a record pace and in an insidious form. At first, a few move into a community, then more and more, then they start converting the local population and when a certain level of 'population saturation' is reached, they start enforcing their laws (Sharia law) and rules on the other peoples of the community. A quick example would be an article out of Scotland where the police of a local municipality created a new 'non-emergency' phone number and, in order to promote it, they handed out fliers with the picture of a puppy, a new recruit to the K-9 unit. Originally, there were reports of outrage by the Muslims in the community, because they consider dogs to be 'unclean'. In this particular instance, the Muslims had not attained the 'population saturation' levels needed in that particular community to enforce their laws, so they've backed off and suddenly they don't have a problem with the cute little canine. But remember my words here when I say that when the numbers of Muslims in that community reach a certain level the puppy on a poster is going to be the least of their (non-Muslim's) concerns.

The next hundred years should prove frighteningly interesting as small nations, not just cities or small communities, reach that 'saturation point', and the men are forced to grow beards while the rights of women are completely revoked and the women themselves are reduced to something akin to slaves. The terrorism of the future is not likely to be 'Islamic Extremist' bombing non-believers, but rather non-believers of all varieties bombing 'Islamic Extremist' in an attempt to regain the freedoms that are very soon to be ripped away from them. It's frightening how the Muslims use the freedoms of speech, etc., afforded them by these communities/nations, to overwhelm the ideals of the free and then oppress them. Usually, by trying to change the local laws and beliefs to the same forms of laws and oppression they fled when they left their homeland.

Based on the information about Muhammad given above, most of which I must admit I learned from research on the internet, am I a bad man for feeling this way? Would anyone who reads this book be a bad person if they don't instantly condemn me? I've never considered myself an intolerant person, but the more I learn about Islam and the other major monotheistic religions the more their followers inspire me with fear.

But our society has become so twisted in its 'Political Correctness' that people of faith of all stripes can proclaim, 'Convert or Die!' with no repercussions while I could end up being ostracized for not believing in their God. Their every example shows their religion to be insidious and dangerous and that it should be banned, yet atheists are seen as immoral.

If you've read this book and at any point thought to yourself that I could be putting my very life at risk by what I've said, then you've already answered the question about whether Islam means peace or not, and simultaneously answered the question of whether or not it should be feared.

> *"I shall cast terror into the hearts of the infidels. Strike off their heads, strike off the very tips of their fingers." Sura 8:12*

They want to end our lives and essentially send us all to hell. Why would it be considered bad to have our military start dipping their ammo in pig blood and burying the Islamic enemy soldiers with pigs carcasses or face down so they can't see or enter heaven? A great many of them believe this would block their souls from entry into heaven and force them to hell. Why should it be ok for them to kill us, ending our lives and, if you believe it, sending us all to hell, and we can't visit that same eternal damnation back on them? American soldiers are to kill the enemy, but are forbidden from doing anything to disrespect that enemy's religion? Ridiculous! These people have all been convinced there is a paradise waiting for them, complete with virgins if they kill us, and although we can kill them back, we're not allowed to block their entry into paradise?

Naturally, I don't believe in their paradise, but they do, and if threatening to rob them of their chance to get into heaven will keep them from killing and murdering long enough for the light of reason to set in, then I say let's get after it. And we wouldn't even have to kill any pigs specifically for the task. I'm sure there are many slaughterhouses from which we could get the required ingredients for a one-way ticket to hell. Now available in liquid gel caps!

I know, it sounds crazy for a person of reason to talk about killing people and burying their bodies with pig's carcasses. How ghastly a threat indeed! And the hope is that it would forever remain simply a threat and never become a reality.

The threat, properly implemented, would save not only the life of the potential terrorist or Islamic Jihadist but the lives of his potential victims and American soldiers. How is that a bad thing?

Of course, the pig blood idea is just a logical device in a thought experiment. One I don't actually agree with and WOULD NEVER ACTUALLY ADVOCATE IMPLEMENTING. Right-wing Christian nutbaggery, if you ask me. It's crazy and disgusting. But, not to defend the right wing Christian nutbaggery any more than I must, it is the kind of thing even rational minds start coming up with when under threat by such a harsh, vile, and insane threat. Your responses and defenses become equally insane.

Both sides die, but only the infidels go to hell (if you believe in such things). If the infidels try to balance this out by following Islam's own rules and adding pig blood to the mix so the terrorist goes to hell, essentially robbing them of becoming martyrs in heaven and taking away all their virgins, the world condemns the infidels for the insult. 'Good' Muslims rage at the victims of their fellow Muslims when those victims resort to methods that are equally damning to the soul of their murderers. Craziness.

But can you imagine the outrage if such a thing were attempted? The Islamic world would simply erupt! Why though? Why would the nice, good Muslims care if bad terrorist Muslim's souls are tainted with pig blood and sent to hell? And why aren't they equally outraged at the terrorist for killing and sending the souls of non-believers and the innocent to hell? Why doesn't the 'peaceful' Islamic world explode about that? The only difference is the lack of pig blood. Well, the reason is that, at least to some degree, they agree with the beliefs of the terrorists and support their ideals. Allah wants Islam to spread and conquer the world. To state anything less is a lie. The terrorists are the true heroes of Islam as they are the ones willing to do the dirty work to make it happen.

Islam is dangerous, start to finish. Muhammad was a murdering warmonger, Islamic law is clearly misogynistic and barbaric, and the followers of the religion have committed and continue to commit heinous and unthinkable crimes. It's an abomination against the intellect of man and, like all the rest, needs to be abolished.

Chapter 8. Good Without God

"I'd be more willing to accept religion, even if I didn't believe it, if I thought it made people nicer to each other but I don't think it does." ~Andy Rooney

Andy Rooney on 60 Minutes

I'm often asked how I can be a goodly person without being a godly person. That's a tough question with a complex answer. It makes me feel good to do good things for other people, and I feel bad when I do bad things and cause others to suffer. I try to live my life to where I feel good and not bad. We've all done foolish, ugly things that keep us awake at night. Whether it be words said in anger or something you've done, we all have tiny holes in our hearts where we've hurt someone else. I certainly have my share, so I try to avoid doing those types of things. I try to extend this level of compassion to all creatures (except spiders).

Why do I not kill people? Haven't had a need to, I suppose. I don't know that I could kill someone unless it was in self-defense. Don't get me wrong, some people just know how to push my buttons and were it not for the fear of doing jail time and shaming myself, there's a person or two I'd probably open up a whole 55-gallon drum of whoop-ass upon... An ass whooping, that's it. A black eye, bloody nose, busted lip type situation. I'd even try to NOT knock out any teeth. Why? Because I don't believe a lifetime reminder for one foolish mistake is a fair bargain. Plus, I'm not a very good fighter, so my hope would be that if I lost they would give me the same courtesy. But lord knows there are quite a few folks who could use a good ass whooping, if you'll forgive the expression. And I'll be the first to admit there are times in my life when I sure deserved one as well. Anytime anyone needs more than an ass whooping. . . call the police, call a lawyer, etc. But certainly, don't try to kill them. They may kill you back.

But to take a life? Ok fine, someone made you mad, but when you end someone you end everything they were ever going to do. Ever! Children and grandchildren they will never have. It's impossible, I suspect, to imagine all the wonderful works of art, music, mathematics and scientific advancements which would have been created by the people who've been slain in the name of the God of Abraham. The contributions the children they never had would have made and their children's children. And those are just the lives lost due to the violence aspect. What about all the people who have died due to advancements in science being smothered by the church? Have you lost a loved one to a disease or illness? If man six thousand years ago had turned his back on theism and embraced science, it's likely, I believe, that those diseases would have long since been cured.

Why do I not steal? Shame mostly. I'm a bad example to use in the stealing department, because I'm one of those people who gives. I'm a giver. If I've got it to spare and you even look like you need something, I'll give it. I've gotten better over the years at not giving away too much. I can't tell you how many times I've given so much or helped so much that I ended up putting myself in a bind. Having to scramble to make ends meet because I helped someone else's ends meet is a burden I've chosen to bear on many occasions. I've always gotten through, but I know I'd be a far richer man if I weren't so giving.

> **"The fact that we live without God is, in a sense, not up to us. It's not really a choice. . . But goodness is a choice. It is the most important choice we can ever make. And we have to make it again and again, throughout our lives and in every aspect of our lives." ~Greg M. Epstein,** *Good without God: What a Billion Nonreligious People Do Believe*

I'm not saying I've never stolen anything. Two instances stick out in my mind where I stole something and got caught and both times were lamentable experiences.

The first was when I was about eight years old. I talked my twin brother into taking a five dollar bill from my older sister's husband. We both got caught, but he had the money on him and took the beating for it. To make matters worse, I didn't fess up to my part in the deed. I got caught with a can of snuff, so I got a spanking and sent to my room. My mom started beating my twin brother with a belt in the living room and she beat him all the way down the hall of the trailer house, into the bathroom and into the bathtub, ripping down the shower curtain before the chaos stopped. My own actions caused so much pain and grief to someone I loved so much that it was unbearable. I knew then and I still know now that no confession from me at the time would have stilled her hand on my brother's back. She would have just finished then turned on me, but that night I learned a hard lesson about the pains of cowardice. Even after getting my brothers forgiveness and my mother's passing, my own self-loathing for the event still affects the course of my life. I'll never be that coward again. I'd rather take the beating than die a thousand times inside for not. That's still one of the worst memories of my life.

The second time was when I was thirteen years old. I got caught stealing tobacco from a grocery store. This time it was my own hand doing the stealing, but I still got caught. The shame of getting hauled out of the store in handcuffs by a policeman and then having my father pick me up from the police station was horrible. In my mind, there is shame in thievery that I find highly distasteful and wouldn't risk it unless I was in the most dire of circumstance.

What gives most people their moral compass? I believe it's due to millions of years of evolving in a communal structure. Our human and proto-human ancestors were pack/herd animals. Even pack/herd animals of today display what we would call compassion when they help or protect each other. From small troops of monkeys, proto-human tribes, early villages, to the modern towns and cities of today, it's clear to see the benefits of helping one another.

> **"If people are good only because they fear punishment, and hope for reward, then we are a sorry lot indeed." ~Albert Einstein**

The same communal structure probably also gave us racism. To protect those like themselves and be leery of those who are different is not something humans invented; it's a phenomenon common throughout nature. The difference is that in nature multiple groups of animals don't tend to intermingle with other races on equal footing like humans have done. And even in those instances where they do, there's not a true intermingling. But animals are just as likely to surprise us with their kindness to other creatures not of their kind.

But wait a second... Who determines what is good and what's bad? Certainly not the evil god monster of Abraham based solely on the moral example given for him in scripture. Our own civilization considers the practices of the ancient Hebrews to be barbaric and heinous, otherwise we'd all have slaves and be marrying little girls. So that God is out.

If I were to ask a professional thief, he may have an entirely different view on the deeds of my childhood. To him, it wouldn't be bad that I was trying to take something from someone else. The act itself would be a good deed in his eyes, getting caught would be where my sin lies.

So as you can imagine, this now becomes the most important question mankind has ever faced. Who determines what is right and what is wrong or what is good and what is evil? Who can claim to cast the divide between morality and immorality? In the modern world, it's clearly the United States of America who has taken up the mantle of defender of the innocent in the name of god. Well, sort of.

I was raised to see the United States as always the good guy and what we were doing was right simply because it was right. At great sacrifice, we brought oppressors to their ruin and freed their people. Then we helped these people recover and brought their standard of living up to our own. At least that's what I thought.

I live a certain life with certain freedoms and luxuries and I wish these freedoms and luxuries on those whom I see as oppressed. The problem with this mentality is some of those who are oppressed actually like being oppressed. Others who are being oppressed hate me and want to kill me because I want to lift their oppression. And still, others who are being oppressed want to see me oppressed so I can be like them. Strangely enough, very few of them actually want to live without their oppression or want to enjoy the same freedoms and luxuries I have. Many will claim they do, then they will come to where those freedoms are enjoyed and they will try to bring the oppression with them. They will flee their home country because the religious there are strangling their lives, and they will move to a secular nation and try to set up the same type of tyrannical rule they fled. This is a horrifying thing to me. I like my version of right and wrong, and I don't want someone to liberate me from my oppression. My oppression? How am I being oppressed? That's just crazy. . . wait a second!

I'M OPPRESSED!!! I just realized! Here is the short list of rights and duties I need someone to come in and help me secure. These rights and duties are given to me by God, as exampled by his prophets.

1. My god given right to marry as many women as I want

2. My duty to kill every man, woman, and male child of my enemies once I've defeated them in battle

3. My right to take the virgin daughters of my enemies as my sex slaves

4. My right to marry little girls

5. My right to cast aside a wife, and thus giving her her freedom, by merely refusing to feed her

6. My right and duty to have a Rabbi suck the blood off my newborn son's mutilated penis

7. My right to stone my teenager to death in the town square if he disobeys me

8. My right to own slaves

9. My right to not suffer a witch to live

10. My right to stone my new bride to death if she's not a virgin

11. My right and duty to destroy anyone who offers up a sacrifice to any god other than mine

12. My right and duty to kill anyone who works on the Sabbath

So you, a believer in the one true God, open up my book and try to imagine how someone who doesn't believe in this crap can be moral? I put forth to you that indeed the challenge has been yours all along. How do you keep from killing people at every turn? When you catch your wife doing the dishes on the Sabbath, what keeps you from picking up the nearest stone and sending her filthy, sinning ass to hell right there on the spot? It must be a terrible burden on you to somehow make your way through our barbaric society filled with civil laws preventing you from exercising certain God-given rights of your faith. In truth, you're only 'good' because the laws of man now outweigh the laws of God in our society. There was a time when the Catholic Church ruled the land and you could murder someone under the charge of heresy, apostasy, witchcraft, or blasphemy almost at a whim. Especially if you were any ranking officer of the church, but the mere accusation alone by one peasant to another of witchcraft or communion with the devil was a death sentence. Often by fire.

So how dare you question the morality of any atheist while clinging to a book dripping with blood and bursting at the seams with rape, incest, and murder, and condones such immoral practices as slavery? You should be ashamed of yourself for propagating such misery on another human being. You are the one whose views of what's right and what is wrong should be questioned. Were it not for the true belief on my part that most of these believers are simply ignorant, I would almost certainly spit in the face of any one of them who would dare to question my morality based solely on the fact I'm an atheist. I wouldn't really do that, of course, because it's nasty. Spitting in someone's face is terribly gross and even if I was wrong about something, I certainly wouldn't want it done to me. Even if I met someone who wasn't ignorant of the evils of God and they questioned my morality, I wouldn't disrespect them so. . . but I might want to. However, I do believe most of these people are ignorant of the origins and atrocities of their own god, and ignorant of the humanistic qualities often associated with atheists. Otherwise, they wouldn't even be asking the question.

Now, it is true there are certain things that only the civil laws of man or cultural politeness keep me from doing, which I would otherwise do without a second thought.

The song, 'I can't drive 55' immediately comes to mind.

Chapter 9. Where Atheist Go When We Die

"The Flying Spaghetti Monster (FSM) is the deity of the Church of the Flying Spaghetti Monster or Pastafarianism, a movement that promotes a light-hearted view of religion and opposes the teaching of intelligent design and creationism in public schools.

The "Flying Spaghetti Monster" was first described in a satirical open letter written by Bobby Henderson in 2005 to protest the Kansas State Board of Education decision to permit teaching intelligent design as an alternative to evolution in public school science classes. In that letter, Henderson satirized creationist ideas by professing his belief that whenever a scientist carbon dates an object, a supernatural creator that closely resembles spaghetti and meatballs is there "changing the results with His Noodly Appendage". Henderson argued that his beliefs and intelligent design were equally valid, and called for Flying Spaghetti Monsterism to be allotted equal time in science classrooms alongside intelligent design and evolution. After Henderson published the letter on his website, the Flying Spaghetti Monster rapidly became an Internet phenomenon and a symbol used against teaching intelligent design in public schools." ~Wikipedia

Touched by His Noodly Appendage
Original artwork by Niklas Jansson

I have some wonderful friends who are Christian and I often get asked what I believe happens to my soul when I die. Some are completely stunned by the idea of there being nothing after death. They can't seem to accept that in my mind when I die, it's just blackness. Nothingness. Many are quick to point out that in their opinion I'm in for a big surprise. Perhaps, but given the alternatives, I think I'd rather choose the blackness. For starters, the descriptions of heaven are very lacking, which is exactly as one would expect considering who wrote them.

We have three possible outcomes when we die. Work with me here, people. If we counted every batshit crazy nutjob out there who thought he knew what happened to the soul post-mortem, it would take volumes just to list the titles. So, in the end, we eventually either go to Hell, Heaven, or my batshit crazy version of nothingness.

You'll notice there's no mention of heaven as we know it in the Old Testament. Even Job, when he's cursing his own birth and wishing himself dead says, 'for now I would be lying down in peace; I would be asleep and at rest with kings and rulers of the earth, who built for themselves places now lying in ruins', which clearly implies he has no concept of the modern idea of heaven.

Therefore, we need to turn to the New Testament for good references to heaven. Go to Revelations 4 in the bible and read the description John gives. It's absolutely hallucinogenic. God sitting on a throne, surrounded by 24 other thrones filled with old men. Then, it describes four rather hideous sounding creatures who do nothing but sing, 'Holy Holy Holy is the Lord God Almighty. Who was, and is and is to come' 24/7, 365 for all eternity. It says so, right there in the bible, so it must be true. So what do the old dudes on the surrounding thrones do every time the four creatures sing praises to God? They fall on their faces and start telling God how wonderful and awesome he is. Forever and ever and ever for all eternity. It says so right there! Apparently, the God of Abraham has self-esteem issues or is quite forgetful of his own awesomeness. And throughout his psychedelic mushroom-induced experience, John mentions zillions of people and creatures and angels and they are all doing one of three things. They are either on their faces praising God, they are killing the people of Earth in the name of God, or they are calling out for the murder of those who are not saved through believing in Jesus Christ.

> **"All national institutions of churches whether Jewish, Christian or Turkish appear to me no other than human inventions set up to terrify and enslave mankind and monopolize power and profit." ~Thomas Paine**

So, where are all of those who died in the name of Christ? Yep, they are with God. Well, sort of. Actually, they are kept underneath the altar that stands before God, where they wait, literally begging God to avenge them. I take this to mean they are begging God to murder people, but they are told to wait until more Christians are slain before they can be released. What? Really?

> *"When he opened the fifth seal, I saw under the altar the souls of those who had been slain because of the word of God and the testimony they had maintained. They called out in a loud*

> *voice, "How long, Sovereign Lord, holy
> and true, until you judge the inhabitants
> of the earth and avenge our blood?"
> Then each of them was given a white
> robe, and they were told to wait a little
> longer, until the full number of their
> fellow servants, their brothers and
> sisters were killed just as they had
> been." Revelation 6:9-11*

Revelation 21 gives us a description of the New Jerusalem, which is said to be new heaven on Earth, and essentially describes a massive cube made out of every precious metal or stone available. A golden city 1400 miles long, wide and tall. Wow, sounds neat. Every building and street made of gold, twelve massive gates around the city, three on each side, each carved out of a single pearl. Twelve levels of foundations and each made of a different precious stone. God really has a thing for gaudy, over the top decor. But I'm guessing the city will be empty.

> *"Nothing impure will ever enter it, nor
> will anyone who does what is shameful
> or deceitful, but only those whose
> names are written in the Lamb's book of
> life." Revelation 21:27*

Yes, it does throw that last bit in there about the people whose name is written in the Lamb's book of life, but how many Christians do you know who are impure or who haven't acted shameful or deceitful? How long do you think you could manage in heaven before doing something wicked or deceitful? The angels couldn't seem to manage very long. What chances do you think you have?

And there's no sun or moon or stars. All the light in the new city of heaven is provided by God. I'm guessing even if you manage to get into the city, chances are good that you're going to spend every waking moment looking at the golden floor as you are on your face praising God. That doesn't sound like a very appealing place or situation. Me and masturbation go too far back to let something as simple as death separate us, so I imagine once in heaven I wouldn't stay there very long, depending on how the evil God monster of Abraham views my fappy time. And what happens to those souls who get to heaven but can't maintain that divine standard? Do you get cast down into the pit of hell for all eternity or do they just toss you out the gates of heaven and let you wander the heavenly ethersphere? Is there a whole universe in the afterlife besides heaven and hell where you can live? No. The way the book is written, the new city of heaven will be a literal place on Earth. This is the end of the New Testament and they still hadn't fully developed their idea of heaven, and it was still a physical place in the physical world. Over time it has developed into an ethereal plane where God and heaven exist.

It's funny that the God created by the Jews, a people mocked for their love of wealth, would create a city made of gold and jewels. Coming from a group of nomadic desert tribesmen, you'd almost expect there to be more water in heaven. We all figure there's no water in hell and, based on the Christian telling of it, there's not much in heaven either, but it doesn't really matter since in heaven you don't get thirsty. My first thought when I read that was, 'I'm going to really miss drinking coffee'.

If you're a Christian and you're thinking to yourself that since I'm an atheist I won't get into heaven anyway so I shouldn't worry myself about their lack of the nectar of the java bean, you could be wrong. In the Old Testament, it wasn't uncommon for God to allow his chosen people to be slaughtered or enslaved by non-believers who went on to be successful and prosperous, solely because the Hebrews either questioned him or didn't follow the rules he wanted them to follow. So it wouldn't surprise me for some of the people in heaven to get tired of doing nothing but telling God how awesome he is and get themselves cast out, and then for God to put non-believers in their places, just to add insult to injury. Cause he's shitty like that over and over again in his own book. Wouldn't surprise me a bit.

But if you're not into golden palaces and would prefer a more tranquil lifestyle in heaven, that's where the Quran comes in. What would heaven be to a group of desert people? How about a lush garden with flowing rivers everywhere? That's sounds good. A river for you, a river for me, everyone gets a garden with rivers. Not a lot of mention of gold, oddly enough. There are some virgin girls tossed in here and there if you died in the name of Allah. That sounds pretty good, unless you happen to be one of the virgins girls. And the idea of 'having' a virgin may sound good, novel perhaps, but I prefer a woman who knows her way around the bedroom. Having to teach 72 girls/women how to have sex could be its own form of hell. 'All these virgins and what I wouldn't give for a single whore,' would probably be my refrain.

> *"Garments of fire have been prepared for the unbelievers. Scalding water shall be poured upon their heads, melting their skins and that which is in their bellies. They shall be lashed with rods of iron." Sura 22:19-20*

Hell is pretty much what you might expect. Lakes of fire with burning and suffering, etc. All the usual suspects, when one contemplates hell. No one wants to go there. You're going to experience every second of the worst pain imaginable for all eternity. But the whole idea of hell is absolutely repugnant when preceded by the words 'Let me tell you about my loving and forgiving God' or 'Allah the merciful'. Merciful my ass! If he so merciful he would merely allow you to vanish to the same nothingness you were before you were born. No pain, no screaming, no gnashing of teeth. Non-believers simply go poof and disappear, rather than being tortured for all eternity.

You love your children, but if they're not home by 10 pm and if they don't constantly tell you that you're great and wonderful and merciful, do you light them on fire? Of course not. What kind of sick shit is that? The entire reason for hell is because heaven isn't attractive enough for us to go through all the time and trouble of worshiping and sacrificing and dedication God requires. If people were given a choice of heaven and hell or the atheist idea of the same blackness as before they were born, there would be no religious people. Describe all the barbaric things you have to do and all the sacrifices you have to make to earn your way into heaven, and even then you might not make it in and won't know until you die, and then tell them about enjoying all the fun the world and the worldly life offers will earn them a painless blackness, just like before they were born, and you'd see an entirely different dynamic in humanity. Without the threat of burning in hell, this would be an easy choice. And if you need the threat of burning in hell for all eternity to keep you from hurting others, then I think some therapy might be required anyway.

The idea of being able to see my friends and loved ones again after death is very alluring, but go and look at the descriptions of heaven in the holy texts. To read the old and new Testaments, it sounds an awful lot like an eternity spent in the pew of a church, and we all know how fun that can be. Even most Christians can't bear it more than an hour and a half a week. Imagine an eternity of you on your face in prostration singing 'Holy holy holy is the almighty God'. At least in hell, it sounds like you get to hop around a bit. Sing show tunes if you're into that sort of thing. It would, of course, be hard to stay on key with all that screaming going on about you, but at least the song would change from time to time.

The Bible actually tells you God will protect you in this life, 'Yea though I walk through the shadow of death,' and yet there's clearly no evidence of such protection. He makes no claims of protection after death, so what makes you think that even if you manage to believe enough in Christ to have your name written in the book of the lamb, you'll be able to stay there? The book of Revelation clearly states no one who does anything wicked will be allowed in heaven, so I suspect that means even after you've made it through the gate any wicked deeds will get you booted. 99.999999% of you can't even follow the rules the Bible lays out for you here on Earth, elsewise we'd have a lot more children being stoned to death in the streets by their parents. Jesus was a Jew and he himself said he was not here to do away with the old laws, and yet very very few Christians actually follow any Jewish practices. When was the last time you, the Christian, celebrated Passover? Jesus did.

And for some reason, you think once you get to heaven there will be peace? Do you think perhaps you'll spend eternity sitting around washing Jesus' feet? John's description of heaven in the book of Revelation shows the armies of heaven being released upon the Earth. Why does heaven have standing armies? And you think these standing armies just sit around for all eternity waiting for this one moment in time to do some fighting? You could argue the armies are there to wage war against the armies of Satan. Good point. Wow, shot me right down. . . Or, you've bolstered my point. There has always been war in the afterlife, where heaven and hell are supposed to exist. A third of the host of heaven; a full third of all the angels and other various creatures who supposedly knew for a fact God and his power were real, rose up against him before man was ever even created. And, based on the heaven and hell battle for our souls, it sounds like the war is still being waged.

The trials of the Israelites are an excellent example that just because God says he'll lead you to the Promised Land, doesn't necessarily mean you'll get there. And even if he promises something to last forever, it doesn't mean it actually will. You can fall from grace. Here's an example:

> *"Now a man of God came to Eli and said to him, 'This is what the Lord says: 'Did I not clearly reveal myself to your ancestor's family when they were in Egypt under Pharaoh? I chose your ancestor out of all the tribes of Israel to be my priest, to go up to my altar, to burn incense, and to wear an ephod in my presence. I also gave your ancestor's family all the food offerings presented by the Israelites. Why do you scorn my sacrifice and offering that I prescribed for my dwelling? Why do you honor your sons more than me by fattening yourselves on the choice parts of every offering made by my people Israel?' Therefore the Lord, the God of Israel, declares: 'I promised that members of your family would minister before me forever.' But now the Lord declares: 'Far be it from me! Those who honor me I will*

honor, but those who despise me will be disdained. The time is coming when I will cut short your strength and the strength of your priestly house, so that no one in it will reach old age, and you will see distress in my dwelling. Although good will be done to Israel, no one in your family line will ever reach old age. Every one of you that I do not cut off from serving at my altar I will spare only to destroy your sight and sap your strength, and all your descendants will die in the prime of life." 1 Samuel 2 27:33

So, they made it to the Promised Land (heaven on Earth for Old Testament folk) and yet there were still rules they had to follow. They had to burn the best of what they had in sacrifice to God and they weren't doing it, so he took away the blessings he had given. Yes, those same blessings where he says he'll deliver you and your family for a thousand generations, or. . . until they stop toeing the line.

And what happens to you when you finally make it to heaven and you're sitting there praising God and you have some kind of wicked thought about a woman? Or what if you are a woman and get to heaven and realize you are a slave? Not allowed to see God directly but to have to stay home and learn from whatever husband you were given to as if you were a cow. A thing to be pent up at home, used, abused, and discarded.

And don't even give me that crap about not being able to think wicked thoughts in the presence of God or I'll bring up that whole 'Lucifer and a third of the host of heaven' thing again. That dead horse just beats itself sometimes. And there's nothing in the bible to refute what I've just said about women getting to heaven and finding themselves in the worst possible situation. Living the horrors little girls in the Middle East are going through to the present day. To the contrary, the Bible is quite clear on the slave status of a woman and on its acceptance of slaves and slavery. In fact, the sheep analogy used in the bible clearly shows the status we're given by this deity. And indeed since the Bible considers men to be the slaves of God, women are even less. A woman is the disposable property of a slave.

Hell, obviously, is not somewhere anyone would truly want to go. Heaven doesn't seem like such a prize either unless you like the idea of spending all eternity in a golden church on your knees worshiping God, or getting raped by suicide bombers. Who knows, maybe Catholic priests also have a line of virgins waiting for them when they get to heaven too. Clearly, not the same virgins, though. Luckily, for the priests, there's a well of these male virgin souls stacking up from all the children God watches starve to death in Africa. Don't worry, priests, I'm sure they're all re-born white and clean in heaven. I'm not racist, so please take that last sentence as it was meant. A slap in the face of those who are white Christian racists and cringed at the thought of their priest getting to heaven and being forced to molest a little black boy instead of a little white boy. Sick bastards on several levels.

I wonder. . . when a male is reborn in heaven, is there a Jewish Rabbi there ready to circumcise him and then suck the blood off the penis? What a fucked up, sick group of pathetic bastards you are to believe this shit! Yeah, I said it! Hopefully, my right to free speech will protect me better than the worthless parents who let these crimes happen to their children. In March 2013 there was news of two infants infected with herpes, and one tested positive for HIV, after being circumcised by a Rabbi with herpes sores on his lips and possibly HIV who felt compelled by his faith to suck the blood off the babies' penises after cutting off their foreskin.

No, I'd rather just die and have everything go black and there be nothingness. I'm lazy, I'd rather do nothing for eternity than spend it on my knees and face as a slave to a merciless God who needs to be constantly told how wonderful and awesome he is. Perhaps going to hell is actually being reborn as a Rabbi who is compelled to mutilate and suck the blood off of little boys' penises.

Yep, rooting for blackness. In fact, I'm counting on it. I accept the fact until proven otherwise, that there is nothing after this life and it's the only one I have. I can squander or enjoy it as I see fit.

My only rewards in the afterlife are the fruits of my actions in life and the legacy I leave behind. Period.

Chapter 10. Slaves and Sheep

"I freed a thousand slaves. I could have freed a thousand more if only they knew they were slaves." ~Harriet Tubman

Harriet Tubman Circa 1885

How quickly the African-American population forgets. For some people, the words 'Never Again' hold a deep and special place in their heart. A people whose identity was once so intertwined with the word 'slave' that even now four or five generations removed from those who suffered such pains the words, 'Never Again', fly from their lips with speed and pride. Then quickly followed by, 'Sweet Jesus, Hallelujah! Praise the lord!'.

Jesus is the slave master and you are the slaves. How can you not see this? The Bible was full of slaves and even tells us how much we should pay for our slaves and how hard we should beat them. Job, during his torment, even wished he could die so he could be like a slave released from his master's whip. And if you prefer to stay with the sheep/shepherd analogy, we can do that. Jesus is the shepherd who protects his flock and you are one of his sheep. Do shepherds and sheep grow old and die together as one big family unit? No. The shepherd shears the sheep for its wool and slaughters the sheep for its meat.

"I am naturally anti-slavery. If slavery is not wrong, nothing is wrong." Abraham Lincoln

You can't really argue that there's no way your soul, the sheep, would ever be harmed in heaven, lest we forget there was a war in heaven. And though there are a few crappy descriptions of heaven for us to choose from with mention of a huge city made entirely of gold and jewels, one has to wonder about slaves in heaven. Oh and there's lots of slaves throughout the Bible. Clearly, God from the Old Testament and Jesus from the New Testament don't have any issues with slavery, so if you're a person of African descent you might be wondering who's back-breaking labor is going to go into building this glorious city. You can't read any vision of heaven in the bible where it's not controlled by an almighty dictator who rules with an iron fist. Why is he going to be merciful to you? And if God and Jesus both believe in the sanctity of slavery, there's no reason to believe your place in heaven won't be under a whip, taking out some angel's trash or mowing his grass, or even picking the heavenly cotton.

"The reason people use a crucifix against a vampire is that vampires are allergic to bullshit." ~Richard Pryor

God or Allah is the worst slave master I've ever heard of. Not only does he demand you do his bidding, but he also demands you constantly give him thanks for everything you've worked your ass off to get. And on top of that, you're supposed to praise him and constantly remind him he's holy and how mighty he is? He's in your mind and knows every wicked thought you have and will burn you in hell for them. He will bring plague and destruction down upon you or your family if you don't follow the above-listed tenants and sometimes even if you do. Not only did he create Satan to tempt and torture you, but he was also thoughtful enough to create hell as well. Be a good, compliant, hard-working slave or you will burn in hell for all eternity.

I don't want to be a slave. I don't like the idea of being a slave in the modern sense of the word, where I have no rights and no freedoms, nor a slave in the afterlife, where rights and freedoms would be the least of my concerns. I like and enjoy the idea that I can go where I want to go and do what I want to do as long as I don't hurt anyone else or curb their right to go where they want to go and do what they want to do. But there's nothing in the Bible stating that once you get to heaven, you'll in any way shape or form be your own master. This holds especially true if you're a woman. I have an entire chapter dedicated to the plight of women due to the cults of Abraham so I won't go into it again in detail here, but it is worth note that the bible explicitly treats women as objects rather than people.

They had rules back then about how long a Hebrew slave had to serve before he could be released. After seven years he was to be set free, but if you gave him a wife and she bore his children he cannot take them with him. He either has to remain a slave to the master for the rest of his life or give up his wife and family. Those ancient Jews sure knew how to screw you with a loophole. Once you have a good slave, give him a wife and let them bear children, then hold his family hostage unless he remains a slave.

"If you buy a Hebrew slave, he is to serve you for six years. But in the seventh year, he shall go free, without paying anything. If he comes alone, he is to go free alone; but if he has a wife when he comes, she is to go with him. If his master gives him a wife and she bears him sons or daughters, the woman and her children shall belong to her master, and only the man shall go free. But if the slave declares, 'I love my master and my wife and children and do not want to go free,' then his master must take him before the judges. He

shall take him to the door or the
doorpost and pierce his ear with an awl.
Then he will be his servant for life."
Exodus 21:2-6

Remember, back then men could have multiple wives so even if he brought a wife with him, he could still fall for this trap. It should also be noted that this rule only applies to male Hebrew slaves. Male foreign slaves are slaves for life.

Here is an example of how, when you as a woman are sold into slavery, you don't have the same time limits provided to the man and are forever the master's slave. You are supposed to please your new master and, if you don't, you'll be given back to your father. This quote from the Bible shows you the only ways a woman can gain freedom from slavery.

"If a man sells his daughter as a slave,
she is not to go free as male slaves do. If
she does not please the master who has
selected her for himself, he must let her
be redeemed. He has no right to sell her
to foreigners, because he has broken
faith with her. If he selects her for his
son, he must grant her the rights of a
daughter. If he marries another woman,
he must not deprive the first one of her
food, clothing and marital rights. If he
does not provide her with these three
things, she is to go free, without any
payment of money." Exodus 21:7-11

So, you're only hope for escape is that your master either marries you or gives you to his son to marry, then your new husband doesn't feed, clothe, or sex you. Only then can you go free. Lucky you. At first, you might think of simply not pleasing your master and being redeemed but it doesn't work because he just gives you back to your father, who almost certainly wouldn't be pleased with you. Without a marketable hymen, he may not be able to marry you off again. If you survived the beatings, he would be within his right to sell you into slavery. That's if we take the word 'redeemed' to mean you were returned to your father. With these death cult barbarians, they could just as easily meant sent to god or otherwise sacrificed. As harsh as these people were, it's ludicrous to think 'redeemed' in the context of a punishment for not pleasing her master would be freedom.

But, by this account, a man only had to feed and clothe a slave only if he intended to have sex with her. Only a married woman, someone he can have sex with, is guaranteed the comforts of food and clothing. He could marry as many women as he wanted and could put them away as easily as telling them he no longer wanted them. He could shame a woman by sending her back to her father, probably to be stoned to death or otherwise sacrificed, or he could simply stop feeding her. If he stops feeding a wife, she is essentially granted her freedom and is no longer his problem. Great for him because he's just dumped a wife, but bad for her because now she has no marketable hymen for a prospective husband, she can't go back to her family, and she has no way to support herself.

If a master chooses to starve his slaves, male or female, or make them go without clothing and they die of exposure, there's no freedom for them. They are to accept it. The only slaves granted those rights are the ones lucky enough to have their masters want to sex them. Foreign slaves have it especially bad as they have no rights at all and there is no end to their servitude. When their master dies, they simply get passed on to the master's children, just like all of his other belongings.

Beatings were quite a common thing back then as were slaves, so naturally there must be rules governing how beatings should be applied to slaves.

> *"Anyone who beats their male or female slave with a rod must be punished if the slave dies as a direct result, but they are not to be punished if the slave recovers after a day or two, since the slave is their property." Exodus 21:20-21*

But whatever you do, don't knock out one of their teeth or cost them an eye. If you do, you'll have to let that slave go and it would be such a shame to lose a perfectly good slave.

> *"An owner who hits a male or female slave in the eye and destroys it must let the slave go free to compensate for the eye. And an owner who knocks out the tooth of a male or female slave must let the slave go free to compensate for the tooth." Exodus 21:26-27*

But surely the warm and fuzzy Jesus, who loves everyone and is the pinnacle of the modern idea of morality, wouldn't condone such actions, right? On the contrary, Jesus is quite plain on his ideas about slavery. Have you ever heard the saying, 'Honor thy father and thy mother'? Well, guess what Jesus says just after that...

> *"Slaves obey your earthly masters with respect and fear, and with sincerity of heart, just as you would obey Christ. Obey them not only to win their favor when their eye is on you, but as slaves of Christ, doing the will of God from your heart. Serve wholeheartedly, as if you were serving the Lord, not people, because you know that the Lord will reward each one for whatever good they do, whether they are slave or free. And masters, treat your slaves in the same way. Do not threaten them, since you know that he who is both their Master and yours is in heaven, and there is no favoritism with him." Ephesians 6:5-9*

Oh Yay! If I'm a good slave in life, I get to go to heaven and be a slave in the afterlife. Jesus does soften up what it's like to be a slave, but that's his whole gig; trying to get people to stop doing so much hurt, but he never condemns the practice and even states plainly we are all the slaves of God. No if's and's or but's. It says it right there in the Bible, you will be a slave. So much for your proud words of, 'Never again!'. Can I get a hallelujah?

> *"Slaves, obey your masters." Colossians 3:22*

In Philemon 1, the apostle Paul writes to a man named Philemon and tells him about a former slave of his named Onesimus. This slave, who is apparently with Paul during his time in prison, fled Philemon's home a gentile, but has become a Christian thanks to Paul's teachings. Paul is sending Onesimus back to Philemon and clearly wants Philemon to release Onesimus from his bonds of slavery and not punish him. It implies he should release Onesimus because he is now a fellow brother in Christ and although he makes it sound like it's a request, it's actually a not-so-subtle command. He opens with stating it's not a command but closes with a reminder of how Philemon owes him a debt.

Christians over time have had differing views on the meaning of this. Earlier Christians took it to mean not to enslave other Christians and more modern Christians try to apply it to all mankind because everyone nowadays knows slavery is bad.

> **"We have the wolf by the ear, and we can neither hold him, nor safely let him go. Justice is in one scale, and self-preservation in the other." ~Thomas Jefferson**

But you know what I think? I think Paul was in prison and he needed his letters carried to Philemon and to others at Philemon's home and Onesimus was the only person available. However, Onesimus was a former slave of Philemon and refused for fear of his former master's wrath. So Paul wrote this letter to gain favor with Onesimus so he would carry his letters for him. Onesimus was probably not there as a prisoner, but as a servant to the prison and had grown weary of the treatment there. He offered up some type of favor for Paul in return for a good word with a former master who wasn't as bad as his current master at the prison. This letter is Paul's attempt to buy favor with

Onesimus for the favor, and although it directly implies one Christian shouldn't enslave another, that is absolutely not a sentiment implied by Christ in Ephesians. Christ was speaking to Christian slaves and telling them to be obedient.

Here's something you may find surprising, God himself sold the Israelites into slavery on multiple occasions for decades at a time.

> *"The Israelites did evil in the eyes of the LORD; they forgot the LORD their God and served the Baals and the Asherahs. The anger of the LORD burned against Israel so that he sold them into the hands of Cushan-Rishathaim king of Aram Naharaim, to whom the Israelites were subject for eight years." Judges 3:7-8*

And again,

> *"Again the Israelites did evil in the eyes of the LORD, and because they did this evil the LORD gave Eglon king of Moab power over Israel. Getting the Ammonites and Amalekites to join him, Eglon came and attacked Israel, and they took possession of the City of Palms. The Israelites were subject to Eglon king of Moab for eighteen years." Judges 3:12-14*

And again,

> *"Again the Israelites did evil in the eyes of the LORD, now that Ehud was dead. So the LORD sold them into the hands of Jabin king of Canaan, who reigned in Hazor. Sisera, the commander of his army, was based in Harosheth Haggoyim. Because he had nine hundred chariots fitted with iron and had cruelly oppressed the Israelites for*

twenty years, they cried to the L<small>ORD</small> for help." Judges 3:1-3

And again,

"The Israelites did evil in the eyes of the L<small>ORD</small>, and for seven years he gave them into the hands of the Midianites."
Judges 6:1

The case for eternal slavery based on the bible is overwhelming. If you're wishing someday to go to heaven, I give you the stern warning to be careful what you wish for.

Ok, one more.

"And because the Israelites forsook the L<small>ORD</small> and no longer served him, he became angry with them. He sold them into the hands of the Philistines and the Ammonites, who that year shattered and crushed them. For eighteen years they oppressed all the Israelites on the east side of the Jordan in Gilead, the land of the Amorites." Judges 10:7-8

Chapter 11. False Prophets

"At that time if anyone says to you, 'Look, here is the Messiah!' or, 'Look, there he is!' do not believe it. For false messiahs and false prophets will appear and perform signs and wonders to deceive, if possible, even the elect."
Mark 13:21-22 NIV

Toufik Benedictus "Benny" Hinn
Image: Public Domain

I find it both funny and ironic that in the above quote, Jesus is talking to his disciples and they ask him about when the end times will come and how to know the signs. It's the normal doom and gloom we come to expect from the returning of the peaceful loving God. In this speech, he mentions false prophets twice and how they will preach falsehoods and lead men astray. Here's the other example:

"Watch out that no one deceives you. Many will come in my name, claiming, 'I am he,' and will deceive many." Mark 13:5-6

It goes on about how those who believe in him will be persecuted and he hopes it doesn't happen in the winter because it will make it even worse. And although, at the end, he does say no one, not he or any of the angels knows when this will happen, only God knows, he does give them a massive hint that everyone seems to overlook. A mind-blowing revelation that should really have indicated to the following generations that Jesus himself was a fraud:

> *"Even so, when you see these things happening, you know that it is near, right at the door. Truly I tell you, this generation will certainly not pass away until all these things have happened. Heaven and earth will pass away, but my words will never pass away." Mark 13:29-31*

He told the people sitting before him that no one knows what day or hour the end will come, but it will happen within their lifetime. Talk about enslaving someone with a mentality of dread. Everything is going to go to hell in a handbasket, the merciful loving God is going to come back and absofuckinglutely destroy everything and there's going to be pain, misery, and death and it could happen at any moment! But it didn't happen. It didn't happen in their generation or the next or the next.

Of course, some of it happened but even Punxsutawney Phil (the groundhog) could have prognosticated those events. Jesus tells them they will be persecuted by other men for preaching against the mainstream religious doctrines of the Hebrews. Duh! So the obvious did happen because later on in this tale of peace and love some of those men do get persecuted, but the supernatural claims are never upheld. I need to get a big red rubber stamp that says, 'False Prophet!'.

It's ludicrous to think the Jews of the day, and even some of the Romans, especially the ones who crucified him, wouldn't be interested to see if Jesus arose from the dead. It was scripture and prophecy he was fulfilling, so surely there would have been quite a few people waiting around to see, but nope. Dropped him in a tomb and went about their day. One of the reasons could be because there were so many people going around at that time claiming to be the Messiah, they had grown numb to the claim. Oddly enough, even the disciples of Christ weren't around when it happened. They had been following this guy and personally listened to his holy words and witnessed his miracles with their own eyes, yet not a one hung around to see him rise from the dead? Maybe people did wait around and it was three days before the people dispersed enough for the hoaxers to get to the body.

In fact, it makes perfect sense none of the male followers are around at all when the women find Jesus' tomb empty. They had already been there, move the stone and removed Jesus' body. For them to now proclaim he had risen would have caused too much direct suspicion, so they either made the women do the dirty work of spreading one of the greatest lies of all of mankind, not an unheard of concept in the bible, or simply had a man there waiting, whom the women thought was an angel. He told them Jesus had risen and to spread the word. My bet is the men were just too cowardly and tricked the woman/women into doing their dirty work.

And even his own followers had a hard time recognizing Jesus after his divine resurrection. Here are a couple of ideas you should consider before leaping to the divine.

1. A replacement Jesus. The inner circle of Jesus' followers took the one who looked the most like him and beat this guy's face and probably punched holes in his hands and feet and gave him a cut on his side. Cut, not stabbed. This would explain why he told his followers to stick their fingers in the holes in his hands. It's not at all unreasonable to think a fervent believer wouldn't willingly step into this role. And I would suspect forty days would be just enough time for infection to set in and him to die from his wounds.

2. What if Jesus didn't die on the cross? What if the Roman soldier didn't kill him with the spear? They got him off the cross, pretended to bury him, but were actually treating his wounds. After the beating, he sustained the swelling which would make him difficult to recognize. Again, with the wounds he sustained during the beating and with their

lack of knowledge of germs, I imagine it wasn't long before infection got him. Just long enough to finish off the hoax.

It's a Roman soldier who stabs Christ to end his life, and when Joseph of Arimathea begs Pontius Pilate, a Roman who didn't want to execute Christ in the first place, for the 'dead' body of Christ, Pilate relies on the word of a. . . Roman soldier as to whether Christ is actually dead. I would be more apt to believe the 'Roman soldier' was either paid off, an imposter, or a convert who helped pull off a hoax, rather than believe the evil God monster of the bible is real.

And one last point I would like to make about Jesus. You often hear Christians proclaiming Jesus died on the cross for us, or that God sacrificed his only begotten son as if these things are extraordinary. Lots of people have willingly sacrificed themselves for any number of causes. Although the examples are many and go back several thousand years, the ones that come to mind the most readily are the sacrifices made by those in the suicide bomber community. Are they not sacrificing themselves for God? Should we not be in awe and wonder that they gave their lives for their beliefs? And there are countless men and women who have proudly sent their children off to die. We can use modern examples of the proud parents sending their children off to die in the service of their nation or we can go back and use more barbaric examples from the Old Testament, where people would literally sacrifice their own children to god.

> *"And Jephthah made a vow to the LORD: 'If you give the Ammonites into my hands, whatever comes out of the door of my house to meet me when I return in triumph from the Ammonites will be the LORD's, and I will sacrifice it as a burnt offering.'*
>
> *Then Jephthah went over to fight the Ammonites, and the LORD gave them into his hands. He devastated twenty towns from Aroer to the vicinity of Minnith, as*

*far as Abel Keramim. Thus Israel
subdued Ammon.*

*When Jephthah returned to his home in
Mizpah, who should come out to meet
him but his daughter, dancing to the
sound of timbrels! She was an only
child. Except for her, he had neither son
nor daughter. When he saw her, he tore
his clothes and cried, 'Oh no, my
daughter! You have brought me down
and I am devastated. I have made a vow
to the LORD that I cannot break.'*

*'My father,' she replied, 'you have given
your word to the LORD. Do to me just as
you promised, now that the LORD has
avenged you of your enemies, the
Ammonites. But grant me this one
request,' she said. 'Give me two months
to roam the hills and weep with my
friends, because I will never marry.'*

*'You may go,' he said. And he let her go
for two months. She and her friends
went into the hills and wept because she
would never marry. After the two
months, she returned to her father, and
he did to her as he had vowed. And she
was a virgin." Judges 11:30-39*

Another false prophet who is certainly worth mention is
Moses of Crete. What? You've never heard of Moses of Crete?
Five hundred years after Christ, this Jewish nutbag convinced
many of the Jews of Crete that he was Moses and was going to
part the sea, so they could walk safely back to Israel. Many of
them cast themselves into the sea but the waters did not part
and, needless to say, many of them drowned. A testament to the
gullibility of the faithful. There are conflicting reports as to what
happened to this Moses, but he either fled the scene or died in
the waters with his followers. Either way. . . False Prophet!

In Qur'an 7:157, it is often understood that Muhammad is claiming that he is the unlettered (illiterate) prophet being spoken of in the Torah and Gospels, but there are tons of problems with this. First off, I don't remember any specific reference in the bible to an unlettered prophet, but it would be easy to imagine most of them were illiterate. Secondly, it's debatable whether Muhammad could read. If he's claiming to be the illiterate prophet from the Torah and Gospels, then he can't read or write, so how did he write the Quran? Divine intervention, of course. But in researching this, his followers proclaimed he was a business owner and was quite literate and educated in their sense at the time, so this disputes the claim he's the unlettered prophet.

But Muhammad was a vicious murderer who ruled by the sword and married children. Things considered not only immoral but quite heinous by our standards today, shouldn't have been moral and sanctioned by God back then. False Prophet!

Joseph Smith was a self-proclaimed prophet back in the 1800s. He proclaimed he spoke with angels and they gave him the power to translate ancient texts. He created his bible called the Book of Mormon and he even took it upon himself to edit the original Holy Bible. As with most 'prophets', all of the tales of miracles performed by Joseph Smith are accounts written by himself or his followers. He got his hands on a scroll of ancient origin with lots of cool writing and pictures on it, so he took it upon himself, with divine assistance, to translate this scroll. He claimed angels helped him with the translation and that it was the lost Book of Abraham. In fact, it turns out the papyrus scroll was actually a copy of the Ancient Egyptian Book of the Dead. Essentially a handbook that tells a soul how to pass through the underworld to the afterlife. Although it has widely been proven to have nothing to do with Abraham or the God of Abraham, the Mormons still worship Joseph Smith's 'divinely inspired' translation. Testament that people will believe anything, even if they know it's not true, simply because they are told to do so.

> **"If religion were true, its followers would not try to bludgeon their young into an artificial conformity; but would merely insist on their unbending quest**

for the truth, irrespective of artificial backgrounds or practical consequences." ~H.P. Lovecraft

The great and powerful Joseph Smith was fond of diddling the wives of his followers. This and the mismanagement of funds for the community he created caused a rift and, he was eventually murdered by those who used to be his flock. He was essentially hiding in a jail in Carthage Illinois when a mob broke in and shot him as he tried to jump out the window. False Prophet!

David Koresh was a colorful character but that's all he was. He goes into a group of sheep and proclaims himself to be a shepherd. He, too, enjoyed sex with the wives and daughters of his followers and, oddly enough, he too had a sense of paranoia. So much so that his teachings and weapons stockpiling gave concern to the neighboring communities. One of his followers turned coat on him and soon after the FBI and ATF went in and burned him out. Lots of killing, lots of death, lots of fire, but oddly enough, no David Koresh rising from the ashes. He's dead and gone but in fifteen hundred years his followers will be singing his praises, talking of his miracles, and murdering in his name. False Prophet!

Jim Jones

Jim Jones led a religious movement back in the '60s and '70s called Peoples Temple, which eventually ended up in Guyana. Apparently, the rest of the civilized world had run him and his group off. On November 18, 1978, over 900 people either committed suicide or were murdered by drinking cyanide, 200 of them children. The coward took the easy way out and shot himself in the head. False Prophet!

Heaven's Gate Cult

A serious loon named Marshall Applewhite led a small UFO cult back in the '80s and '90s. He preached a half Christian, half UFO type religion where the earth was going to be 'recycled' and the only way to survive was to kill yourself so your soul could catch a ride to heaven on a spaceship, which was trailing the Hale-Bopp comet. In March 1997, 39 people, including Applewhite, drank a cocktail of poison, laid down in their cots and covered their upper torso with a square purple cloth. With $5.75 in their shirt pockets for the intergalactic fare, they put a bag over their own heads, just in case the poison didn't work and died. Two former members committed suicide in similar methods afterward. But wait! The comet came and went but the earth wasn't recycled and we're all still here. What's up with that? False Prophet!

"Religion was invented... when the first con man met the first fool." ~Mark Twain

There are some more modern examples of false prophets. Joel Osteen, Pat Robertson, Benny Hinn, the list goes on and on. Go on the internet and watch the antics of these nutbags or their ilk and tell me you don't think they're in it for the money. There have been news crews document the healings of Benny Hinn and it's plain to see he won't let anyone with a real illness get near him. It's all a bunch of hocus pocus to get you to give him money. And I dare him or any of them to challenge me on this. Meet me at a hospital of my choosing and let's see some miracles. I doubt they'll even bother suing me for calling them frauds. To do so would elevate public awareness of my book, plus I would then challenge them to prove their claims. If they can't prove their claims under scientific scrutiny, then it's not slander or libel to call a fraud a fraud.

The same type of shysters and lowlifes who were tricking poor people out of their money and possessions thousands of years ago are still doing it today. I'm sure any one of these batshit crazy asshats would enjoy the comparison to Jesus Christ, even if it is in a derogatory sense. Any time anyone claims to know the mind or word of god, they should be immediately institutionalized and deprogrammed. Oh sure, it sounds mean for me to say such things, but for people of reason to institutionalize and educate those of faith in today's modern facilities would be absolute paradise compared to the institutionalization performed by the faithful and the torturous treatments they've inflicted on atheist throughout history.

False prophets have been around since the beginning. There were other people going around Jerusalem at the same time as Christ, performing miracles and claiming to be the Messiah. Now, just like then, they are nothing but a bunch of crooks trying to get your dollars or sheep or goats or whatever. Rubber stamp all these televangelist asshats and throw them all in prison forever.

So say we all!

Chapter 12. In God We Trust?

"Religious institutions that use government power in support of themselves and force their views on persons of other faiths, or of no faith, undermine all our civil rights. Moreover, state support of an established religion tends to make the clergy unresponsive to their own people, and leads to corruption within religion itself. Erecting the 'wall of separation between church and state,' therefore, is absolutely essential in a free society." ~Thomas Jefferson

Thomas Jefferson
Painting by Rembrandt Peale (1778–1860)

Much debate has gone on about the separation of church and state in the U.S. and many believers are quick to argue that the founding fathers were Christian, and therefore the United States of America is a Christian nation, but this is patently false. In fact, on several occasions, it's expressly stated that the U.S.

supports no official religions. There are no temples or churches in government buildings for a reason. The instant you officially sponsor one religion, you immediately begin officially sponsoring religious segregation and persecution against all the other beliefs. An example would be having all the atheist and Muslim kids go stand in the hall during the pledge of allegiance, because it contains the words 'under God' and not everyone believes in that god. This happens now even though there isn't an officially sponsored religion. If the government is allowed to sponsor a religion, we'll start having prayer time and bible study and creationist obfuscation science taught in our classrooms. And where are the atheist and Muslim kids going to go when all that is going on? How long is it after the United States officially sponsors Christianity before I have to say the Lord's prayer in order to get my driver's license? How long before they start making me proclaim my belief in their lord and savior Jesus Christ before they'll let me have a business license? Prejudice comes in many forms. You might be surprised to know that in these free United States where we personify the American dream of being able to be anything you want, it is against the constitutions of eight states for an atheist to hold public office.

> **"The president says he speaks to God every day and Christians love him for it. If he said he spoke to God through his hair dryer, they would think he was mad. I fail to see how the addition of a hair dryer makes it any more absurd." ~Sam Harris**

Eight state constitutions that ban atheists from holding public office:

Arkansas: Article 19 Section 1

"No person who denies the being of a God shall hold any office in the civil departments of this State, nor be competent to testify as a witness in any Court."

Maryland: Article 37

"That no religious test ought ever to be required as a qualification for any office of profit or trust in this State, other than a declaration of belief in the existence of God; nor shall the Legislature prescribe any other oath of office than the oath prescribed by this Constitution."

Mississippi: Article 14 Section 256

"No person who denies the existence of a Supreme Being shall hold any office in this state."

North Carolina: Article 6 Section 8

"The following persons shall be disqualified for office: First, any person who shall deny the being of Almighty God."

South Carolina: Article 17 Section 4

"No person who denies the existence of a Supreme Being shall hold any office under this Constitution."

Tennessee: Article 9 Section 2

"No person who denies the being of God, or a future state of rewards and punishments, shall hold any office in the civil department of this state."

Texas: Article 1 Section 4

"No religious test shall ever be required as a qualification to any office, or public trust, in this State; nor shall anyone be excluded from holding office on account of his religious sentiments, provided he acknowledge the existence of a Supreme Being."

Pennsylvania: Article 1 Section 4

"No person who acknowledges the being of a God and a future state of rewards and punishments shall, on account of his religious sentiments, be disqualified to hold any office or place of trust or profit under this Commonwealth."

And Many Christians in America think it would be all well and good because they think the government is going to sponsor the same god they worship, and they are right. . . for now. But in some cases, religious conservative nutbags are trying to make the case that although the federal government shall make no law respecting an establishment of religion, or prohibiting the free exercise thereof, they believe the states should individually be allowed to support a specific religion, in both the state offices and in the schools. In April 2013 some conservative legislators in North Carolina put forth the following resolution.

> GENERAL ASSEMBLY OF NORTH CAROLINA SESSION 2013 H D HOUSE JOINT RESOLUTION DRHJR10194-MM-54 (03/19) Sponsors: Representatives Ford and Warren (Primary Sponsors). Referred to:
>
> *DRHJR10194-MM-54*
>
> A JOINT RESOLUTION TO PROCLAIM THE ROWAN COUNTY, NORTH CAROLINA,
>
> 1 DEFENSE OF RELIGION ACT OF 2013.
>
> SECTION 1. The North Carolina General Assembly asserts that the Constitution of the United States of America does not prohibit states or their subsidiaries from making laws respecting an establishment of religion.
>
> SECTION 2. The North Carolina General Assembly does not recognize federal court rulings which prohibit and otherwise regulate the State of North Carolina, its public schools, or any political subdivisions of the State from making laws respecting an establishment of religion.

Do you know what they are trying to do? They are trying to subvert the First Amendment of the US. Constitution. The same right-wing religious conservative nutbags who think the Second Amendment is so precious are quite eager to thumb their nose at the First Amendment.

Amendment I

Congress shall make no law respecting an establishment of religion, or prohibiting the free exercise thereof (and then it goes on blah blah blah free speech, blah blah blah, etc)

One of the catches, though, is that if a state can bypass the federal government and support a specific religion, they can also officially prohibit the exercise of any religion they choose. If they can separate themselves from the 'Shall make no law respecting an establishment of religion' part, what keeps them from separating themselves from the 'prohibiting the free exercise thereof' part? Just numbers. All they need is the right amount of religious saturation in the members of the state's legislating body. So what if the legislators in North Carolina get what they want? Where does it stop? They can pass laws requiring an hour of Bible study a day for every student. Is it going to be a Catholic Bible study or Protestant? Southern Baptists in the south, of course. Technically, they could then make it against the law to not go to church. You could get fined for not tithing enough. They could pass laws against apostasy, atheism, and blasphemy. What would keep them from passing state laws and arresting people at will for simply not believing in the right god? You say to yourself, 'Well, we had 'under God' in the pledge and 'In God we trust' on our money for years and none of those things happened,' and that's true, those bad things I just mentioned didn't happen. Because we had that pesky First Amendment protecting us. You want your Second Amendment rights to bear arms and need my support to keep it? Deal! You just promise to help me keep my First Amendment right not to have the government officially forcing your God down me and my family's throats.

> **"Our civil laws have to comport with a higher law. God's law." ~Sen. Rick Santorum**

And another problem with the idea of each state being able to support a particular religion is what happens when a state with a high Muslim population such as New York decides to officially sponsor Islam instead of Christianity. When suddenly Christian children are asked to stand in the hall while the words, 'Under Allah' are said in the pledge of allegiance? How are the Christian parents going to take it when their children are mandated by law to study the Quran for an hour a day at school? All state government employees required to bow and pray five times a day. Christians violating state law and having to stand before a Sharia court? I doubt you'd be very happy.

During the cold war and hence, the term political prisoner was commonly heard throughout the media. If states are allowed to pass laws allowing individual support of a state religion, will the term religious prisoner find its heyday? Do we start having prisoner exchanges between states where a Christian state expels all its religious prisoners to an Islamic state and vice versa? If New York becomes an Islamic state and there's a female virgin on death row for a heinous crime, such as refusing her arranged marriage, will we have a prison guard forcibly rape her to satisfy the rules against executing a virgin in Islam? Not uncommon in the Middle East, where God and government are highly intertwined. In a twisted, vicious, godlike manner it makes sense. I mean, why waste a perfectly good hymen?

Does each state start printing its own currency with its preferred deity on it? How long is it before we have states refusing trade with other states based on religion? The legislators think they are doing God's work and they are right. God is a destroyer and this move brought to its fruition would destroy the unity of the United States and turn us into the truly fascist state these same legislators claim to hate.

> **"As a Christian, I have no duty to allow myself to be cheated, but I have the duty to be a fighter for truth and justice."**
> **~Adolf Hitler**

The founding fathers wouldn't have supported this. They would have supported the time-honored tradition of slavery and the oppression of women, but they would have never supported states independently passing laws for or against the religion of its choice. This example of religious conservative douchebaggery is blatant and will surely be stopped, but some religious oppression can be insidious in its various forms.

"We should create law based on the God of the Bible." ~Sarah Palin

Religious oppression is the clear reason why the people fled England in search of a new life on a faraway continent. Now, admittedly, a good many of the original settlers were one brand of belief or another, but they were being bullied and slaughtered by the believers who held a majority in England, so they fled. They desired to find a place of peace where they would be the majority and they could be the ones doing the bullying and the slaughtering.

The founding fathers of the United States Constitution specifically avoided any mention of a preferred God throughout their formal documentation, in an attempt to avoid causing the same religious oppression and persecution which drove the people to flee England in the first place. Over the years between the American Revolution and the Civil War, the Christian religion had grown due to its insidious nature and the fervent efforts of its followers. It spread like the plague it is and when the horrors of the Civil War brought many people to the doorsteps of the church looking for salvation, it gave the religious movement the strength it needed to push its way into our government. An act of Congress on April 22, 1864, was the first shot across the bow of the freedom from religious persecution. That was the day Congress passed an act allowing the words, 'In God We Trust' to be stamped on our coins. I wonder how civil rights leader and atheist Susan B. Anthony would have felt about that. She looks quite angry on the coin...

Susan B. Anthony US Dollar Proof Coin

"I distrust those people who know so well what God wants them to do, because I notice it always coincides with their own desires." ~Susan B. Anthony

This is all well and good as long as you're a Christian, but it seems to alienate everyone else. Many Americans would be absolutely disgusted if, 'In Allah We Trust' were written on our money. You think it's ok for my atheist son to be forced to say the word God in the pledge of allegiance, but to have your child be forced to say 'One Nation Under Darwin' or 'One Nation Under Allah' and you would be livid! You would be beside yourself with rage and indignation. You would refuse to handle the money or you would pull your children from that school, so why should I have to handle money with your God on it? Why should my child be singled out and shamed and made to go stand in the hall, just so your child can say God in school? And don't start with the whole founding fathers were Christian bullshit either. It doesn't work.

You want the Ten Commandments on the courthouses? Why? Ok, the Ten Commandments can be found in Exodus 20 so let's check them out.

1. You shall have no other gods before me.

2. You shall not make any graven images (Catholics take note)

3. You shall not take the lords name in vain

4. Remember the Sabbath

5. Honor your father and your mother

6. Do not kill

7. Do not commit adultery

8. Do not steal

9. Do not bear false witness against your neighbor

10. Do not covet your neighbor's property

There are your precious commandments. Have you ever wondered why they stopped there? Well, technically, they didn't. God spoke these commandments and the Israelites became fearful and backed away from the mountain. The narrative pauses the recitation of the commandments to inform us of this, and then god continues with his commandments. I could list them all here, but they do tend to go on a bit. I'll point out some of the more interesting ones.

"Anyone who attacks their father or mother is to be put to death" Exodus 21:15

"Anyone who curses their father or mother is to be put to death." Exodus 21:17

"Do not allow a witch to live." Exodus 22:18

"Anyone who has sexual relations with an animal is to be put to death." Exodus 22:19 (Walking a thin line there, Oklahoma)

"Whoever sacrifices to any god other than the lord must be destroyed." Exodus 22:20

"Do not blaspheme God or curse the ruler of your people" Exodus 22:28 (Obama hating right wing tea bags take heed)

And these aren't even including the commandments concerning slavery and the treatment of women. I address those issues in other parts of the book, but thought they were worth mention here as well. Did you notice the passage where God tells his chosen people to destroy whoever sacrifices to any God other than the lord? Yes, right there, two chapters after your precious ten commandments he tells you to destroy (kill or otherwise persecute and ruin) anyone who sacrifices to any god other than him.

C'mon, you want your ten commandments, well there they are, alongside a few others you may have never heard of or simply chose to ignore. Go to Exodus 20 and start reading if you doubt me. Switch up between the newer understandable versions and the literal translation versions for fun. I know, it's crazy to think of actually going and reading the bible for yourself, but go ahead. I'll wait. . .

So what did Moses do after receiving the hefty list of commandments from God? Rednecks are going to love this. They threw a huge barbeque! They did it just like we do it in Texas.

"He got up early the next morning and built an altar at the foot of the mountain and set up twelve stone pillars representing the twelve tribes of Israel. Then he sent young Israelite men, and they offered burnt offerings and sacrificed young bulls as fellowship offerings to the LORD. Moses took half of the blood and put it in bowls, and the other half he splashed against the altar. Then he took the Book of the Covenant and read it to the people. They responded, "We will do everything the

LORD has said; we will obey." Moses then took the blood, sprinkled it on the people and said, "This is the blood of the covenant that the LORD has made with you in accordance with all these words."" Exodus 24:4-8

Well, not quite how we do it in Texas. We don't normally spread the blood all over the place. Imagine Middle Eastern desert people with camels living in tents and an older Jewish man dressed in robes calling forth the young men of the tribe to sacrifice some bulls. There are dead bull bodies lying around, they capture the blood and then Moses himself starts praying and chanting to God as he sprinkles the blood all over the altar. And this is seen as a good thing in God's eyes. God's favored, leading by example. It's like a scene right out of a movie about devil worshipers and zombies, without the pentagram. Real animal blood, not this fake water or wine crap that modern religious people use and claim is symbolic blood. Then he takes this real animal blood and sprinkles it on the people as they recite something right out of an Orwellian dystopian sci-fi horror movie where all the people have been taken over by some form of evil mind control. This is fucking ghastly!

It would be hilarious if we could get a bunch of atheists to show up at a mega-church parking lot before service and reenact the above sacrifice. When the police show up we can explain that since it's a holy ritual they can't stop us, but they're free to drag up a sacrificial bull and join us if they like, as long as their penises don't have foreskins, of course. We could always offer to circumcise them there in the parking lot, but I doubt they'd take it in the spirit we intend it.

These are the beliefs and actions of the people you look to for your moral guidepost? No wonder you stop at ten. And why should anyone who doesn't believe your faith be forced to follow these rules? You are a Christian and want the ten commandments carved into a huge stone monument at your courthouse, because there is this secret, back of your mind hope that either god will watch over the proceedings or, and this is more likely, the people doing the judging will keep these commandments in mind. You live under the illusion this nation was created by a bunch of Bible thumping evangelical Christians, and you seem to keep forgetting how dangerous a popular vote democracy can be when the majority believe in a murderous God and the government and military support that God. It's amazing how all the right-wing conservative nutbags are actually praying to God to turn the United States into Iran. How ironic.

And how comfortable would you be if we removed the Ten Commandments and put the rules of Sharia law, Islamic law in stone? What if 'In God We Trust'were replaced with, 'There is only one God and Muhammad is his prophet' on your money? It's coming, or could be.

Sharia law is now being practiced in Sharia courts in England, so what's to say it won't happen here in the U.S.? It's just a matter of time before the population saturation of Muslims is high enough. How many of you Christians were raised up and had no idea Muslims even existed? I was raised with no idea of what Islam was or a Muslim, but with the help of some terrorists attacking us on our own soil, mosques popping up everywhere, and honor killings finding their way into our cities, it's now hard to not know. And their religion is spreading like any other plague or infestation. It won't be long before there are issues in the U.S between Muslim and Christian cities/states. I don't care what brand of nutbag you are, Agnostic, Atheist, Christian, Jewish, Muslim, Wiccan or whatever, you should call me a nutbag and then join me in protecting the First Amendment and keeping God, all of them, out of our schools, local and state governments.

Oh, and it's almost too petty to mention, but I thought I'd toss it in here at the end of this chapter... If individual states can ignore the first half of the First Amendment, then they can also ignore the second half. You know that pesky blah blah blah free speech stuff I mentioned earlier? That's right. You could lose your right to bitch about protecting your right to bear arms! Then where would you be?

God bless 'Merica!

Chapter 13. Watch Your Tongue

> "Mockery of religion is one of the most essential things... one of the beginnings of human emancipation is the ability to laugh at authority." ~Christopher Hitchens

Christopher Hitchens (1949-2011)
He was the first man among us. A great light has gone out.

Many people simply don't know the difference between a heretic, an apostate, and a blasphemer, so I thought I would help clarify. Back in the day, in order to determine if someone should be stoned to death, beheaded, or offered up as a burnt sacrifice, you needed to know in exactly what fashion the perpetrator had offended God and then dole out the proper execution.

Apostasy is when you renounce your faith and teach directly against your former faith. I was raised a Christian, but I've turned away from that cult and I will now actively teach against it. By that definition, I am an apostate. Words and phrases I use can be considered blasphemy, but we'll get to blasphemy in a bit.

Heresy is when you believe in the same God as the main doctrine but teach a different form. For example, the Hebrew people used to sacrifice animals to God as redemption from sin. Jesus was a Jew and believed in the same God, but he was teaching that many of those sacrifices were no longer necessary. By that definition, he was a heretic and some of the things he was claiming were blasphemous to the Jewish establishment.

Heresy is different from apostasy in that a heretic still believes in the same God as the main doctrine, where an apostate does not. By definition, anyone who doesn't worship at the same church you do, and by that I mean doesn't worship God the same way you do at your church, is a heretic. Anyone who leaves Christianity for Islam and starts preaching the Islamic faith could be considered either a heretic or an apostate, depending on whether the person making the accusation believes the Muslim God is the same God or not. But a Christian who believes everything about Christ except the notion that Christ and God are the same being, could be considered a heretic and for him to teach his belief would be heresy and blasphemy.

How many people do you suppose have been murdered for heresy and apostatizing throughout history? The number, of course, is unknowable but with all probability, it's quite large. And we haven't even covered blasphemy yet.

> **"I don't believe there is such a thing as blasphemy, just outrage from those insecure in their own faith" ~Stephen Fry**

The Merriam-Webster Online Dictionary defines blasphemy as:

1. a: the act of insulting or showing contempt or lack of reverence for God
    b: the act of claiming the attributes of deity

2. Irreverence toward something considered sacred or inviolable

Blasphemy can be committed by anyone and almost anything can be taken as blasphemy. It really depends more on the person making the accusation of blasphemy and how narrow their views. Sometimes, blasphemy is blatant and intentional, such as the entire content, or at least the intent of the entire content, of this book, but other times it can be accidental or inadvertent. In fact, Jesus committed blasphemy by claiming to be God and demanding people worship him. Although he didn't see it that way, it's almost certain that's how the Jews of the day would have taken it, and fully explains why they went to the Romans, who were the law of the land at the time, and asked for Jesus to be arrested and executed. And even if you disagree with my assertions about whether Jesus claimed to be God or not, it's really quite irrelevant. The point is that Jesus was a Jew teaching things other than the main Jewish doctrine and therefore he was a heretic.

George Carlin, blessings be upon him, was a model blasphemer. His blasphemy was so perfect I could almost claim he was divinely inspired. He said it best when he said:

> **"Religion has convinced people that there's an invisible man ... living in the sky. Who watches everything you do every minute of every day. And the invisible man has a list of ten specific things he doesn't want you to do. And if you do any of these things, he will send you to a special place, of burning and fire and smoke and torture and anguish for you to live forever, and suffer, and suffer, and burn, and scream, until the end of time. But he loves you. He loves you and he needs money." ~George Carlin**

Now, George Carlin, blessings be upon him, was a controversial individual in many areas of his life and the public arena during his time, and I think he would enjoy the irony of my giving him the traditional 'blessing be upon him' type salutation. Primarily for the fun it pokes at those who continuously spew this 'my God has a small dick and must constantly be reassured of how wonderful he is' crap, but also because it's just fun. That entire last line would be an excellent example of blasphemy. And George, if you're out (down) there. . . Try hopping around, buddy. I heard it helps.

Christianity and Islam by their very existence are blasphemous to Judaism. Islam is heretical to Christianity because it teaches a different version of the message of the Abrahamic God. Judaism and Islam also deny the main tenet of Christianity, which is that Christ is God and was raised from the dead. The Jews see him as a false Messiah and the Muslims see him as just a prophet. This would have to be one of the most heretical and blasphemous things a Jew or Muslim could say to a Christian and would explain many a death. But this isn't any more blasphemous than telling a Jew not to offer up burnt offerings to cleanse away his sins. He might see it as Satan trying to trick him into losing his soul to hell by not following the covenant of sacrifice. By the same token, Christianity outright denies the divinity of Muhammad's teachings altogether and many see him as the false prophet Jesus was warning his followers about. Religion is an all or nothing game and everyone loses. Cults draw up their lines of state like small nations unto themselves. It's no wonder they war with each other. And they can't even agree among themselves within one particular religion, let alone trying to get three completely opposing ideologies to come together. They are all heretics and blasphemers to each other, and the blood of the innocent and non-believer runs free while they battle over which one follows God the right way. It's pathetic, it's barbaric and I'm hoping the civilized man will grow to shun it in its entirety.

"I see Atheists are fighting and killing each other again, over who doesn't believe in God the most. Oh, no... wait... that never happens." ~Ricky Gervais

Ricky Gervais
Publicity shots for the 2010 Golden Globes
Courtesy of www.rickygervais.com

Thanks to the Greeks and Romans, Christianity, especially Catholicism, is more of a pantheon than a proper monotheism. The Greeks and Romans believed in many gods so in order for the 2nd and 3rd century Christians and early Roman Catholic Church to fill the gap, they had to come up with their own demigods; icons to fill the place of such notables as Mercury and Pan, Zeus and Apollo. At first, it was hard for the pagans to imagine how one God could do everything where before it took a pantheon, but the early Christians reasoned a way. They invoked sainthood upon Jesus' disciples and various others and started using angels and these saints as replacement idols for the old gods. They were eager to attribute certain functions, positions, or powers formerly held by the old gods to God, Jesus, angels, and saints. Zeus is replaced by Yahweh, Apollo replaced by Jesus, Mars replaced by the Archangel Michael; Hades replaced by Lucifer, the list goes on.

Saints are more about the day to day stuff, and people often believe a specific saint watches over them based on what profession they've chosen, or where they were born, or by the saint their parents named them after. St. Jude is the patron saint of little children, so millions of people will kneel down and pray to this saint for help in healing sick children, despite the fact God specifically says not to offer prayers to anyone but him. Millions of Christians all over the world wear crosses and worship stone statues of these angels and saints despite the commandment, one of the big ten, specifically stating NOT to worship graven images and stone statues.

All of it, every dot and tittle, is heresy, blasphemy, or apostasy from one viewpoint or another. If the Holy Bible is the true and infallible word of God, and if you're not following the absolute word of God with absolute devotion, then you're just picking and choosing which rules you want to follow and thus you are doing it wrong. You are a heretic and a blasphemer, period. There should be Jews stoning their children to death on a regular basis. Jesus was supposed to be the Messiah who would unite the twelve tribes of Israel and rule the world, but it didn't happen, so unless you have proof, real proof, that Jesus did any of the things attributed to him, especially his resurrection and divinity, then you really should be a Jew. Unless you have proof any of Muhammad's supernatural claims are true, you should also be a Jew. Come on, Muhammad split the moon in half and jammed it back together, surely we should see evidence of this. The argument that there's no sign on the moon of such treatment because Allah put it back together so perfectly doesn't hold for one glaring reason. Muhammad split the moon for the explicit purpose of proving his power and relationship with Allah, so one would think the scar would remain as proof to the following generations. Wacky crazy that logic stuff.

The only problems with this line of thinking is if the Christians and Muslims can't prove their prophet's divinity, they should be Jews, and the Jews have no proof their god is real either. Hahahaha! And you people are afraid of a few atheists? Yes! Although we are the group least likely to kill you, we're also the group most likely to undermine your faith and prove you a fool. Be very afraid.

"All great truths begin as blasphemy."
~George Bernard Shaw

In today's world, we have so many different variations on every different religion that the heresy and blasphemy must drip from this planet as if from a blood-soaked sponge. There are a few people who try to follow the law of their faith to the letter, but even in those groups you still have. . . groups! Yes, groups! There's not one official 'original' way it is to be done. Each has their own interpretation of the words of some misogynistic, slave trading, crotch cricket riddled sheepherders and tentmakers who lived in the ancient desert. You do have some Jewish groups who try to follow the Torah to the letter and some Christians who try to do the same with the Bible, and of course, we can't forget the Muslims. They all have groups who try to follow even the most eclectic rules of their faith and even these groups within groups can't agree on the right way to worship God.

So who's to know the right, true, and proper way to worship God? Often times, I've asked Christians and they, as did I when I was among them, think everyone but Christians is going to hell. And even some of the other Christians were going to hell too because they weren't doing it right. Hell is a very open-minded place, where everyone is welcome and apparently where everyone is going. I have this vision in my mind of the golden streets of heaven all quiet and empty, with the exception of the occasional tumbleweed blowing by; God sitting on his golden throne, all alone, lamenting the fact the made the rules too hard. Oops, more blasphemy on my part. Shucky darn I'm gonna burn.

> *"O you who believe! Take not the Jews and the Christians for your friends and protectors: they are but friends and protectors to each other. And he among you that turns to them for friendship is of them. This friendship makes any Muslim an enemy of their own and deserving of the same fate as the unbeliever. This is because God does not guide an unjust people." Sura 5:51*

So, in the end what you have is heretics and blasphemers all, and they spend their time and energies killing each other under the pretense of heresy and blasphemy. And they do it in the name of the loving and merciful God. Makes perfect sense. But, in my opinion, to refer to the evil God monster of Abraham or his prophets as loving or merciful is quite profane. And unless someone can prove the existence of God and his sanctioning of a specific religion, then I think anyone who makes the claim someone else has committed heresy or blasphemy, the accuser should suffer the punishment the accused would have received. Maybe then we'd have a lot fewer deaths caused by these nutbags. The Salem witch trials are a good example. The mere accusation of witchcraft by little girls leads to death. What a small-minded group of folk.

Heretics all and damn the lot of them.

Chapter 14. To Turn a Phrase

"What a piece of work is a man, how noble in reason, how infinite in faculties, in form and moving how express and admirable, in action how like an angel, in apprehension how like a god! the beauty of the world, the paragon of animals"
~Hamlet Act 2 Scene II

William Shakespeare (1564-1616)

I love the English language. It may seem an odd notion to some people, but to me, it's a rather amazing thing that one creature can formulate an idea in their mind and then express that idea in such a fashion as to where another creature can understand it with perfect clarity. That alone is an amazing feat, but then when you start adding the colors and nuances afforded us by a rich and diverse language things really start getting interesting. There are many languages on this planet, and I'm sure all of them are riddled with religion to one degree or another, but in this section, I'll be talking about English.

A good book can make you laugh or cry. It can have you sitting on the edge of your seat with excitement or fear, or it can twist your stomach into a nervous ball with anticipation. It can draw your mind in so much and so deep that you become completely oblivious to the world around you. If you're a younger person, you may see books as video games for old people. Fair enough, at least you get the point. Being such a fan of language and an opponent to religion, you'd think I'd have a fairly straight forward opinion on the matter, but I don't. I'm a little torn because religion is so ingrained in our vernacular that there are some things which can't quite be expressed without it. There truly are times in my life when I feel blessed, for lack of a better term. See, that's my point! It just doesn't have quite the same meaning if I say today I feel truly fortunate. Truly lucky? But even though you know I don't believe in God, if you heard me say I felt blessed, you would understand the emotion I was experiencing; the chemical reaction going on in my brain.

 You have a new girlfriend in your life and your job is going great and it's difficult to find the words to express the warm, fuzzy, glowing feeling you get when you reflect on such things, so you turn to words we've used since childhood. You may be a little more narcissistic than I and have a feeling of pride and achievement rather than any sentiment of gratitude, but I think you get the point. Of course, the theist is going to maintain that you should be grateful to God for those things and that warm fuzzy feeling is God showering you with his love, but I feel this is unfair. First of all, religious nutbags from all various religions and cults can whip themselves into a frenzy of emotional 'warm and fuzziness' for just about anything, so just trust me when I say that feeling is something you're doing to yourself, no God needed. Fellow atheist, and much smarter person than I, Sam Harris is a neuroscientist and is probably the person who can tell you what chemical interactions are going on in your brain that make you crazy. But to take away all the credit for your own hard work and give it away to God, who put in no discernible effort, to me, is like tossing a good steak out to a lazy dog. You got up every morning and put your shoes on and went to work and made a good showing of yourself, so you earned that promotion. Your girlfriend didn't show up out of nowhere by God's command. No, you had to woo her yourself… and you did it. All by yourself! Go you! I hope she's naughty, those are the best!

 But because the emotions of gratitude and guilt have been hijacked by religion, it's second nature to reach for those familiar words we've depended on since childhood. You may feel blessed that you found this book or you may feel sinful and dirty for reading it. There was a time in my life when I was an early teen I tried to switch from using the term, 'God damn' to 'Devil damn' because I felt dirty swearing while using God's name in such a fashion. I must admit, I also had hoped in the back of my mind that God would find favor with me for cursing the devil all the time. It's wasn't as catchy as 'God damn', so it never stuck. Nevertheless, religion has either hijacked or spawned all the really fun words. Sinful, dirty, unclean, wretched, sacrifice, sovereign, wicked, the list goes on.

But in my case, this limited ability to express myself is due to being raised a Christian and from always falling back on these expressive terms to convey important emotions or ideas. When you learn a friend is in the hospital and you don't know if they're going to live or die, what words of consolation do you give the family that compares to, 'I'll pray for you'? Telling someone they'll be in your thoughts or that you wish them well just doesn't quite cover it. With time, I'll get used to giving someone my condolences rather than offering prayers, but condolences simply don't offer the verbal hug I'm trying to give. I won't fake offering prayers. In my opinion, offering prayers to the God of the Bible to heal someone who is sick or injured is like asking the driver of the truck that ran over them in the first place to back over them again.

I've admitted to enjoying the added flavor religion brings to a language, to a degree, but cultism is a pervasive and dangerous thing. It gets in your hair, your clothes, your bedroom, your wallet, and your mouth. Even those of us who've turned away from the beliefs have an adjustment period where we have to relearn how to think and what to say. Many times I've wanted to say I feel blessed when something good happens because there's not really a secular word that covers it. But I've held back or used a different word because I didn't want the misconception I was a believer. Being raised Christian, it's hard to fight the urge to offer prayers for the sick or damn something when I'm angry, but it will come with time. Giving up praying wasn't so hard since I never mastered its nuances anyway, but giving up damning things is going to take some serious effort on my part. Well, not so much the damning, I don't really swear very much, but the whole blasphemy thing is just too much fun to walk away from.

Human beings are good at recognizing patterns, especially patterns as obvious as sneezing being associated with illness and death. One might imagine the significance of a sneeze during the times of the plagues, so it's no surprise whatsoever that the various religious cults around the world have given to blessing someone who sneezes. But there are many different words from many different cultures addressing a sneeze, many or most of them have nothing to do with God, but rather wishing someone good health.

When someone sneezes, do you bless them? Do you know why you bless them? I'm an anti-theist and there's a 50/50 chance I'll bless you after you sneeze. Why would I do that, you ask? I might do it without thinking, it may simply be polite or, and this is my favorite, if someone knows I'm an atheist, I'll do it simply to have a laugh. My humorous blasphemy when I was younger was all about the funny. If it hit my brain and I thought it would make someone laugh, even if it was just me, I would say it. There was no mal-intent, but as I've grown and watched the horrors these people visit upon each other over a god which none of them can prove exists, my humor has become pointed and sometimes derogatory.

The way religion has wrapped its way into our culture, it's no wonder it's so hard to purge it from our language. Many times, I don't even try. If someone calls me before 5 am, you'll most certainly hear me chastising them for knocking me from my bed at such an ungodly hour. And heaven help them if they do it again. There may be some cursing and the word hell is almost certainly going to come into play. I may even damn the person, if they really make me mad. But the idea of thanking God for everything I had or constantly praising him and telling him what a good, loving God he was just never quite took in my mind. If I was running low on cash and a check came in the mail, I was never really one to refer to it as a 'godsend' as I've yet to receive a check from God with his name on it that I could deposit in my bank for work I didn't do.

I have refrained from most uses of religious terminology, but sometimes it's just too much fun and I can't help myself. I try to refrain from saying things like, 'Thank gawd my team made it into the playoffs' or 'god must really hate the Dallas Cowboys to let so many prayers go unanswered.'

'Thou shalt not eat of an animal with a cloven hoof. It is unclean. But I can eat it all day long, so pass me the bacon!'. Language is fun, and using the language of sanctimonious assholes against them is just that much more fun.

My father was a Christian, but he had a great sense of humor and didn't take the faith too seriously most of the time. He would quote his own scriptures like, 'Thou shalt not leave dad in the car for two hours at Wal-Mart. Book of Mickey, chapter nine, verse four.' When I was a teen, his language tended to be colored with things like, 'Heaven help you. When we get home' followed by the usual attempts to pull the demons out of me or to send me back to the fiery pit from whence I came… mom. Those are difficult humorous sentiments to properly express without the words of religion.

One of my favorite signature jokes is when I see a woman with a troublesome child, I'll suggest she rock her child to sleep and then offer to go get the rocks. This always got a good laugh because there's nothing that smacks of funny like joking about stoning your children to death. I didn't actually come up with that joke; I stole it from my Christian dad.

When you mix blasphemy and comedy, the sky's the limit. When I originally wrote this chapter I was going over the rough draft of this book with my girlfriend at the time and she was sitting next to me. Her little dog, Bailey, jumped up in my lap and while I was petting it the little thing just insisted on licking and it was driving me crazy. Finally, I took the dog's cute little head in my hands, looked her in the eyes, and in my sweetest tone of voice, I told her that if she licked me one more time I was going to offer her up as a burnt sacrifice. Me and my girlfriend glanced at each other and started laughing. Of course, the dog had no idea what I said and just got more exited and 'licky' as we humans laughed. My girlfriend said, 'Jesus!' and pushed Bailey off the couch because she was tired of me and Bailey going through the licking thing. Then she shook her head, leaned back against the couch, laughed and exclaimed 'God!'

Both of those expressions on her part were not related to this book or chapter, even though she had been reading the draft. They were natural expressions which found their way into her language during her Christian upbringing and, despite her current Wiccan belief, she still employed them out of habit. I bumped her with my elbow and said, 'Neither one of them had anything to do with it,' and we had another laugh.

She and I used to do this kind of thing all the time. Once, she said there was a bleach stain on her sweatpants and it looked like Jesus. I immediately proclaimed I was a believer and said we need to cover her up with a burka. She said, 'You think so?' and without missing a beat I said, 'No one said you could talk!' We hee-hawed.

So, I can't really say I'm against religious talk but that doesn't mean I subscribe to or believe in their teachings. I still might say, 'Holy shit!' when I'm startled, but that doesn't mean I believe in religious fecal matter, especially that which is spewed at the altar every Sunday. Of course, the devil is in the details so I guess it would be more concise to say that I enjoy the words religion has brought into the English language as long as they are not actually being used in the practice of the religion. Heaven knows it's a godforsaken world in which we live, so where would we be without the words to express it.

May Thor help us!

"It is not the strongest of the species that survives, nor the most intelligent that survives. It is the one that is most adaptable to change." ~Charles Darwin

Charles Darwin (1809-1882)

Definition of Theory:

1: the analysis of a set of facts in their relation to one another
2: abstract thought: Speculation

Merriam-Webster Online Dictionary

One of the problems we have today is the misunderstanding of the definition of the word 'Theory'. A scientific theory is an idea based on a set of facts. Darwin's theory of evolution is just exactly that. An idea based on the observation of a growing set of FACTS in their relationship to each other. Many people in their ignorance take the word 'theory' in the title 'theory' of evolution and intentionally imply the meaning of the word is speculative guesswork, even though they know that's not the case. These same people also misquote

Darwin and display their ignorance by saying 'Survival of the fittest' when the actual intent of the statement is survival of the one with the best ability to adapt.

There is currently a war being waged against reason and an assault upon the intellect of mankind has been launched. New Earth Creationists take the bible very literally in many respects, and they believe the Earth is between 6000 and 12,000 years old. Some become downright insulted by the idea of evolving from primates as if the idea makes them somehow 'dirty' or less of a person, yet oddly enough they're quite eager to compare themselves to sheep. They make foolish arguments like, 'Well, if we evolved from monkeys, then why do we still have monkeys?'. This is a weak-minded attempt to fool themselves into thinking they have an arguable position, a brazen display of ignorance of the facts. Clearly, we didn't evolve from the same monkeys we have today. Humans and the apes we have today evolved from the same ancestor. Somewhere along the way, one group of apes went one direction and evolved into humans, while the rest of the apes, their equivalent of right-wing, gun-loving, Christian conservative nutbags, thought that whole 'walking upright' thing was unnatural and against God's law. They shunned the opposable thumb as the work of the devil and proclaimed, 'If there is no God then why does my fingertip fit perfectly inside my nose? If there is no God then why does this banana fit perfectly in my arse?' and chose to not evolve.

Creationists will also look to junk science or twist real science to try to back up their arguments. One of the most ignorant arguments they will try to use is the 2nd law of thermodynamics, which states that in a closed system eventually the energy will be dissipated and therefore life could not have evolved on earth because all the energy in the system would have been used up. But the earth isn't a closed system. We have the sun which constantly pumps massive amounts of energy into our atmosphere every second of every day. The 2nd law of thermodynamics argument could be applied to the entirety of the universe in that eventually the energy within will be used up but when working on such a vast size and time scale, it allows plenty of time and energy for the development and evolution of life. When they're finished displaying their ignorance of the 2nd law of thermodynamics, ask them if they know any of the other laws of thermodynamics.

They will often misquote Darwin and either claim he recanted his work on evolution and the origin of species, or that he converted to Christianity on his deathbed. All of this is patently false. They will also take things he said in the ignorance of the age and quote him as if those things he said were still true today. At one point, Darwin lamented the fact that there wasn't very much evidence to support his theory of man's evolution from ape. This fact was due to the lack of scientific exploration of the day. Over a hundred and sixty years later and we have found mountains of evidence to support his theory of natural selection. If he were alive today, he wouldn't make such statements. And he even said with time the needed, evidence might be found, and it certainly has been.

> **"You will be greatly disappointed (by the forthcoming book); it will be grievously too hypothetical. It will very likely be of no other service than collecting some facts; though I myself think I see my way approximately on the origin of the species. But, alas, how frequent, how almost universal it is in an author to persuade himself of the truth of his own dogmas." ~Charles Darwin**

Theists often quote a letter Darwin wrote (above) and imply that he didn't believe the theory of evolution could explain the origin of species. This is a narrow-minded and deliberate twisting of his intent. He was saying he thinks he may have found the origin of species, but all too often an author will believe what he's writing whether it's true or not. At the time, there wasn't much in the way of evidence and Darwin admits this with the first line in the quote, but much has changed in the century and a half since Darwin. The evidence is there at nearly any museum for you to go and ignore in person.

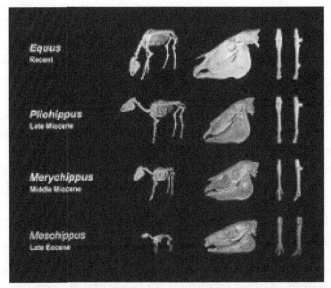

Equine evolution. Composed from Skeletons of Staatliches Museum für Naturkunde Karlsruhe, Germany.

I could have put the monkey/human skeletons, but everyone has seen those and they've been done to death, if you'll pardon the expression. Above is a nice progression of horse evolution. We don't just have proof of human evolution; there are examples of the evolution of thousands of different species littering museums all over the world.

It would help if people actually knew what a theory is and the difference between a hypothesis, a theory, and a fact. Let's start with defining a fact. Let's pretend I have a red light bulb and that is our fact. You come along and you see my light bulb and you ask yourself how this particular light bulb became red. There is no doubt in your mind the light is red. The question becomes 'how' the light became red. You don't know, so you make a few guesses.

1. Someone got cut and bled all over the light bulb

2. The light bulb was painted red

3. A magic fairy used her wand to change the color of the light bulb

4. An invisible man who lives in the sky willed the light bulb to be instantly made red.

Ok, at this point you've made several guesses. Each of these guesses is called a hypothesis. You see something, wonder why it is the way it is, and then you start making educated, well hopefully educated, guesses as to what may have caused what you've observed. You don't see blood anywhere else in the room, nor red paint, so you need to take a sample and send it to the lab. You scrape off some of the red from the bulb for analysis. You don't see any magic fairy dust around which would be indicative of fairy work and if God made it red with the snap of his fingers, the sample you sent to the lab should prove quite interesting.

So when your analysis returns and you discover the red coating is a brand of paint produced by DuPont, you can eliminate three of your hypotheses. A complete lack of hemoglobin tells you it's not blood, the lack of fairy dust tells you no fairy was involved, and since there were no deity dyes involved you can presume God didn't paint it. So now three of our hypotheses have been discounted and we are left with a theory.

A key point to remember is that just because you believe something, doesn't make it true. An extension of that thought would be: Simply because a majority of the population believes something, doesn't make it true. There was a time when a majority of mankind believed the world was flat. . . need I say more?

> **"Eat shit! 10 trillion flies can't be wrong."**
> **~Bill Maher**

The Theory of Evolution is one of the favored battlegrounds of the creationists. They have keenly honed their ability to blatantly ignore the most obvious examples put before them while still crying out, 'Show me the evidence!'

So, we have a Homosapien skeleton and parts of a skeleton from a Sahelanthropus tchadensis 'ape', the creature people are generally referring to when they say we came from apes. The creationist points out the missing gap and claims that since we don't have the skeletons to fill the missing gap between the two examples, the theory of evolution is flawed. They claim the lack of evidence is evidence for the proof of God as the creator. There's a missing link and without that bit of evidence, they claim, the entire theory of evolution collapses. Then we present the skeletal remains of Australopithecus africanus; a creature which fits perfectly between the Homosapien and Sahelanthropus tchadensis. Do they concede their position? No. They point out the gap between Homosapien and Australopithecus africanus and the gap between Australopithecus africanus and Sahelanthropus tchadensis and again maintain the gaps are evidence against evolution. So we present the remains of Homo erectus and Ardipithecus ramidus to fill those gaps and now what do we have? Two ends and three links in the middle? No, according to the creationist, rather than seeing five pieces of evidence supporting the theory of evolution they see four gaps where god must have stepped in. The scientists find the skeletal remains to fill a gap or 'link' and rather than giving any ground at all, the creationist arrogantly proclaims now there are merely more gaps to fill. This is a never-ending argument. No matter how many pieces of evidence we have, there is always going to be a gap.

When we turn a keen eye from scrambling to fill the gaps on our table of evidence to the table of evidence put forth by the creationists, we find they have no real proof of their own. Their claims are as silly as, 'The world was created as a place perfectly suited for man to thrive and therefore an intelligent designer must have created it.' This is preposterous. We should take all the people who make this claim and dump their ignorant naked asses in almost any environment on the planet with none of the helpful technologies of science and civilization and see how long they last. Of all the universe, the earth was created perfectly suited for man, so if we take a thousand of these nutbags and drop some in the desert and some on a barren island and some in Antarctica and some in the wilderness all with no clothes and no tools, they should every single one make it out safe and sound right? The rationality of my response can be equal in proportion to the arrogance and ridiculousness of your original claim. But science is helping debunk this argument more and more every day. Beyond the obvious example I just mentioned for the earth not being the perfect place for man, there have been discoveries of other planets in the galaxy possibly capable of supporting life. Poof! There goes another creationist 'theory' up in smoke.

Lunar Eclipse
InSapphoWeTrust from Los Angeles, California, USA

"The Church says that the earth is flat, but I know that it is round, for I have seen the shadow on the moon, and I have more faith in a shadow than in the Church." ~Ferdinand Magellan

And what are the theists going to think if we ever make contact with another sentient species? I'm sure this reaction will vary but you can almost bet if we ever intermingle with another species, the religious nutbags of our world will spill their blood. Whether it be because they see the aliens as the work of Satan or because the aliens deny the truth of the existence of their God, either way, there will be bloodshed. The evil God monster of Abraham is a fan of blood. And as I postulate in the chapter on anti-theism, it would be an excellent reason why we've not been officially and publicly contacted by an extraterrestrial species. Our religions scare them. I would not be surprised to learn the earth was under quarantine until the religious infestation has been removed.

I saw a cartoon picture on the internet once of an alien ship that had landed in a field and these three-headed aliens approach a farmer and one of them says, 'We mean you no harm. Have you heard of our Lord and Savior Jesus Christ?' Quirky, yest, but can you imagine an event such as this would certainly give an atheist like me a moment of pause, but it is extremely unlikely this would be the case. If alien contact is made and they are theists, it is going to make for one very interesting world in which we live. If they believe in one God, then the monotheist of this world and theirs may try to reconcile the two. We would be right to hope they don't worship an evil God like the God of Abraham. Imagine a technologically advanced Islamic type civilization armed with the weapons that would surely come with such advancement, and the kill or convert mandate of such religions. They could wipe the non-believers out from space. All of them.

Some people talk of feeling God's presence wash over them, most often when being led by a rousing or emotional sermon, and they claim that to them it's proof of God, but in reality, it's another testament to the wonders of the human brain. You get yourself so psyched up and foaming at the mouth for whatever voodoo you're practicing and your brain starts flooding with all manner of chemicals. It could be Buddhism, Hinduism, Judaism, Voodoo, Witchcraft, whatever; you'll find people in all those groups who claim to feel the same sensations. Those same warm and fuzzy feelings Christian people describe as 'having the spirit wash over them'. You see Christians in their churches or Muslims in their mosques and they get all riled up and excited in their love of God or Allah, shaking about, chanting, some of them crying and wailing, and they are absolutely convinced they're in the presence of the Lord. They can feel it, it's God right there washing over them, but it's not. It's nothing more than mental masturbation. It's a semi-self-created delusion. I say semi-self-created because there's usually a holy man of one fashion or another stirring up the fervency and helping you get your delusion on, but he's not required. Even a moderate believer can wind up their personal delusion in the comfort of their own home.

Creationists like to bring up real science, like DNA and the understanding of the human eyeball, and drop in God's hand anywhere there's a gap in understanding. Unfortunately for them, their God of the gaps is getting smaller and smaller all the time as advances in science expand man's understanding of the universe. Darwin's own notes have been twisted and used to argue against evolution.

> **"To suppose that the eye with all its inimitable contrivances for adjusting the focus to different distances, for admitting different amounts of light, and for the correction of spherical and chromatic aberration, could have been formed by natural selection, seems, I freely confess, absurd in the highest degree." ~Charles Darwin**

There you have it. Charles Darwin calls evolution absurd. Not just absurd, but 'absurd in the highest degree'. It's a done deal, evolution debunked by Darwin himself! We can all go home! But wait… the creationist is really hoping you'll not go look up the rest of the quote...

> **"When it was first said that the sun stood still and the world turned around, the common sense of mankind declared the doctrine false; but the old saying of *Vox populi, vox Dei* (The voice of the people = the voice of god) as every philosopher knows, cannot be trusted in science. Reason tells me, that if numerous graduations from a simple and imperfect eye to one complex and perfect can be shown to exist, each grade being useful to its possessor, as is certainly the case; if further, the eye**

ever varies and the variations be inherited, as is likewise certainly the case; and if such variations should be useful to any animal under changing conditions of life, then the difficulty of believing that a perfect and complex eye could be formed by natural selection, though insuperable by our imagination, should not be considered as subversive to the theory. How a nerve comes to be sensitive to light, hardly concerns us more than how life itself originated; but I may remark that, as some of the lowest organisms, in which nerves cannot be detected, are capable of perceiving light, it does not seem impossible that certain sensitive elements in their sarcode should become aggregated and developed into nerves, endowed with this special sensitivity." ~Charles Darwin

I can see it now… when the quote miners get ahold of this book. "Right here Chris Mallard says, 'There you have it. Charles Darwin calls evolution absurd. Not just absurd but 'absurd in the highest degree'. It's a done deal, evolution debunked by Darwin himself!' so even Chris Mallard knows Darwin didn't believe in evolution." And this is exactly what they try to do to Darwin's work. I use quotes and scriptures throughout this book, but I try specifically to not quote people or scripture out of context. Scripture is so violent and ugly I don't have to do any creative cutting as it often convicts itself.

It's a done deal though, evolution debunked by Darwin himself! When it comes to the theory of evolution and natural selection I'm a dyed in the wool believer. When it comes to the history of mankind before four or five thousand years ago, I have a hard time swallowing some of the things I'm told. I believe in evolution, but I'm supposed to believe men and women, just like the people of today, walked this earth for over a hundred thousand years and never did anything with themselves, then suddenly BANG the great pyramids? Look at the advancements we've made in the past two thousand years...the last two hundred years! Mankind went from the first flight of an air machine to landing on the moon in sixty-six years and yet we're to believe men as intellectually capable just sat on their thumbs for over ninety thousand years? There's evidence to suggest mankind had reached surprising levels of civilization over ten thousand years ago. Most mainstream scientist will argue the evidence is false and the way things are taught is the way they are. Other scientists want to know if there are gaps of understanding we're missing and search to discover what juicy little tidbits of knowledge those gaps may hold. So to one degree or another, we all have our issues with the mainstream establishment.

Other scientists, or at least people claiming to be scientists, will use arguments like irreducible complexity to try to disprove evolution. DNA is too complex to have evolved; the human eye is too complex to have evolved, etc. These arguments are specious at best. Falling back on the small and shrinking God of the gaps argument. It is true indeed that DNA and the human eye are complex, but just because we don't know exactly how they developed doesn't instantly grant the existence of an all knowing, all seeing creator. And you have to be careful when basing your God on the gaps of scientific knowledge in today's world, because those gaps are getting smaller and smaller. Scientists are finding life of various forms in places formerly thought to be too harsh and cruel for any creature to exist and yet there it is. Life! They are called extremophiles and they live in toxic or acidic environments or in places of extreme temperature, such as thermal vents on the ocean floor. These creatures have proven life can exist in harsher environments than the cold of empty space and the heat of reentry which would have been required for life to have come here from another planet. There are any number of hypotheses and theories better capable of explaining the dawn and progression of life on earth than an invisible sky god who crossed his arms and blinked everyone into existence.

> **"I have never seen the slightest scientific proof of the religious theories of heaven and hell, of future life for**

**individuals, or of a personal God."
~Thomas Edison**

And to disregard the evidence in the name of faith is exactly what they want. Of course, they are going to tell you that! That's the big test! The best slave is a mindless slave. To have faith Jesus died on the cross for your sins and to have faith in God/Allah and Christ/Muhammad regardless of the scientific evidence against their existence or the crazy violence taught in their books. To follow the horrible moral examples set forth by their books even though your own morality tells you it's bad. To have faith Allah really wants you to cut an infidel's head off with a pocket knife and post it on YouTube. It all takes faith. The type of beliefs and morals you would expect from people who lived a harsh desert life.

You are an eternal slave to a make-believe God! Once you accept that fact, you will be free.

Chapter 16. The Morals of God

> **"Kill a man, one is a murderer; Kill a million, a conqueror; Kill them all, a God." ~ Jean Rostand**

Jean Rostand (1894 - 1977)

Are we more moral than god? I often hear the argument that we can't label Muhammad as a pedophile, even though he married a girl when she was six and let her scratch the dried semen from his robes until she was nine, when he finally bedded her.

> *"Narrated 'Aisha: I used to wash the semen off the clothes of the Prophet and even then I used to notice one or more spots on them." Sahih Bukhari 1:4:233*

That's when he finally started having sex with her, because she was finally old enough and that's how things were done back then. That was considered moral and acceptable to society. Why do we not see it as moral and acceptable now? How can we take anything they said as just and moral if any one thing they did we find so abhorrent?

If Jesus said it's ok to have slaves as long as you don't beat them more than they deserve, then why don't we have slaves? Because it's immoral, of course, therefore Jesus was immoral. Why is it immoral today but it was perfectly legit during the time of Christ or the time of the Old Testament? The argument is made that times are different and society has changed our morality. This is a good argument, but not for the side of God. This is an excellent argument for the advancement of civilization away from the horrible teachings of the various blood cults of Abraham, but not a very good argument for how the people back then were acting. If our morality now is closer to the way God intended than that of the original Israelites, he would have said so in the Old Testament. The Old Testament and the teachings of Christ would have been filled with tales of how slavery is bad, how you shouldn't have sex until you're over eighteen, how it's wrong to murder your own children, and that you shouldn't murder people and cut their foreskins off to give to someone else as a present. If God is all knowing and knows the beginning from the end and the end from the beginning, then he should have picked up on that whole 'thou shalt not screw little kids' commandment most civilized nations uphold nowadays and perhaps at least have mentioned it.

> **"I was in the death struggle with self: God and Satan fought for my soul those three long hours. God conquered - now I have only one doubt left - which of the twain was God?"**
> **~Aleister Crowley**

In the chapter about women, I mentioned the story of the Levite who gave his new wife to a horny hoard of homosexual Hebrews in order to save himself. Well, we get another example of the morals of God further along in that story. The good Israelites, the ones who destroy the town of Gibeah and kill the Benjamites, number over four hundred thousand in the beginning. According to the Bible, they go up to God himself and he personally tells them to attack so they do, and they lose almost fifty thousand men trying to take the city. The armed men of Gibeah number just under thirty thousand and are all wiped out and every person living in the city is killed so there's probably another thirty thousand when you count women and children. Around a hundred thousand people slaughtered total.

In the battle for Gibeah, on the first day the Lord God himself sent the tribe of Judah against Gibeah. They set up camp just outside the city and waited. The Benjamites came out and kicked their holy asses. The Israelites lost twenty-two thousand men with no mention of loses by the city defenders. On the second day, they attacked again with the same result, directly urged on by the very word of God himself. This time they lost eighteen thousand, again with no mention of loses to the Benjamites. That's forty thousand Israelites slain in the first two days of a siege God himself commanded them to lay, against an army of less than thirty thousand. Then on the third day, the Israelites, tired of getting their asses handed to them, did the same thing, but this time they started using their brains. They set up camp outside the city as before but when the Benjamites came out to attack, the Israelites fought for only a moment, then fled. They led the attacking Benjamites away from the city so an ambush force could slip in and 'put the sword' to the remaining unarmed inhabitants and set the city on fire. The Benjamite army saw the smoke from their city behind them and fled to the mountains but they were all hunted down and killed. Over a hundred thousand dead and an entire city razed, all for the life of one girl. A girl the male 'victim' of the story turned out to her murderers. It's odd how the closed doors that protected him after he turned her out to the horde weren't strong enough to keep them at bay without her sacrifice. There's probably some interpretation of the story somewhere where the rape and murder of the woman is her own fault; punishment for running away from her arranged marriage to an abusive husband.

And for all we know, the Levite could have just had an argument with someone in the city, killed his concubine himself and merely accused the Benjamites. History is rife with tales of murderers dismembering their victims. It's quite a gruesome thought that the hero of the story, the one who called for justice, felt compelled to personally cut his bride into pieces and mail her body parts across Israel. The same bride who had already shunned and shamed him once, found herself cut up and mailed across Judah. This would also explain why the Benjamites would risk total destruction rather than turn over a few men. There was no one for them to turn over. No one committed the crimes for which they were accused. Can you just imagine God apparently sitting on the hillside laughing his ass off as Israelite slew Israelite by the tens of thousands?

If time travel ever becomes possible, I think the first thing we should do is go back and get video evidence proving the stories of God in the Old Testament were just the imaginings of a band of desert dwellers. Although the video evidence of no god actually present in the Old Testament would mean the rest of the Abrahamic religions are based on a lie, it would still be requisite to go back and watch the crucifixion of Christ and then record it when the followers of Christ pull his body from his tomb and pull off the greatest hoax of all time. Then we'd naturally have to go spend some time proving Muhammad's claims were false. We'd probably want to get a blood or urine sample while we're there so we can test it for indicators of a brain tumor. I suspect some of the things about Muhammad are true, such as his headaches, hallucinations, hot sweats, etc. His talks with angels were probably the result of tumor-related hallucinations or some other cerebral malady. Once we've done all this, we should then banish the worship of these death cults forever. Their capacity for destruction and harm is unlimited.

> **"Those who can make you believe absurdities can make you commit atrocities." ~Voltaire**

Back in the day, they had no idea what was going on in the natural world, so they attributed almost everything to God. Life was grueling and tragedy struck hard and often. A sickness, an earthquake, a flood, a plague of locusts. . . Yes, I said a plague of locust. It's absolutely not unheard of to see locust or grasshoppers or other insects come together in a breeding, feeding horde. They come, they eat, they sex, and they go. No miracle there. All this stuff happens all the time. Thanks to the internet and the media, we get to watch it happen-then-pass on our TVs or computers. But back then, they attributed these things to God as if he were directly punishing them. Any nutbag walking around crying out, 'You're not following God and bad shit is going to happen to you' is going to be right sooner or later. You ever notice no matter how much time the ancient Israelites spent with God nor how many miracles they must surely have personally witnessed, he always had a hard time keeping them on track? At the drop of a hat they would start worshipping golden calves or questioning the manner in which they are supposed to talk to God or deny him altogether. It sounds like they didn't believe. Why would they have a hard time believing? Because he wasn't there! People in the group wrote down the things that happened to these peoples and dropped their God into the stories.

The first temple was a garden built in Jerusalem. After wandering for years in the desert setting up their tabernacles in tents, they decided to build a temple in the city. Like the Persian kings of the day, it was much like a garden and the king of the people was personally responsible for its care and maintenance. One of these kings, Zedekiah, fell in politically with the Egyptian Pharaoh Hophra and rebelled against the Babylonians. Babylonian king Nebuchadnezzar II defeated the Egyptians sent to protect Jerusalem and then laid siege to the city. When he finally took the city, he destroyed the temple and banished the Israelites from Jerusalem. A short time later, someone writes the story of how God had created paradise, not man, and then God created man and put him in the role of caretaker of the garden. This man was tempted by the serpent (Hophra) to be a true king and not a puppet of the Babylonians. This was the information gleaned from the tree of knowledge of good and evil. The other Jews tried to warn him against rebelling, but he did it anyway and paradise was destroyed. The whole story of Adam and Eve can't even jokingly be considered a description of the origins of man. It's a part metaphor and part history and all bad penmanship.

And to claim the timeline on this line of thinking is wrong because the Adam and Eve story was written before the fall of the first temple is merely guesswork. There's no evidence to back up the claim Genesis 1 is any older than any of the other texts. It's more logical to presume a survivor of the destruction of the first temple, someone who had read the other books and knew the stories and names of the people in them, wrote the Adam and Eve story than it is to believe the content of the story itself.

And the entire story of Jesus is a repeat of a theme. Throughout the Bible, I mean from the absolute very beginning, men and women see the miracles and terrible might of Yahweh first hand and yet they either disobey him or doubt him time and again. Here again, God presents himself to the Jewish people, not just through words and deeds but full-blown miracles, yet they deny him. They disobey him and they doubt him and then they crucify him. And just like in the Old Testament, God is going to punish them for not believing.

There were a few who had heard of the Persian and Egyptian mythologies and they stole bits and pieces where it suited them and their story. Just like the people of today and throughout history take a religion presented to them and change their lives to better follow this religion, they also tend to worship by their own interpretation and thereby change the religion to suit their own desires. All the fractures and different sects, churches, and branches of the various Abrahamic religions are perfect examples of this phenomenon. The Catholic and Protestant divide quickly comes to mind as an example of a group of people who felt they had a better understanding than the orthodox teachings and wanted to express their faith in a different manner or method. Notice how, as the harshness of life fades thanks to the advancement in technologies, the harshness of the God being worshipped also fades. Modern day Christians living a comfy life in middle America have this warm and fuzzy idea of a God who loves them, thinks they each and everyone are special, and he's going to cuddle with them in rays of sunshine when they die. The idea of burning an animal alive, or even dead, in direct worship to that God is absolutely repugnant to them, but that's the kind of twisted, abhorrent behavior the evil God monster of Abraham loved and saw as holy.

Of course, it's an understandable fact to any intelligent person that a creature capable of creating the billions of galaxies in our universe, the trillions of stars, the planet earth, and all of humanity would naturally get off on the cries of a screaming goat and subsequently the smell of its burning flesh. It really doesn't matter that Jesus said not to do it anymore, the very fact God wanted it in the first place tells us God's true nature.

And we must remember that Jesus was a Jew. Everyone knows of the last supper where Jesus ate with his disciples but what was so important about this meal? I'm sure they ate together all the time, but the reason this meal was so special was that it was Passover. It wasn't special because they knew Jesus was about to be crucified; it was special because they were celebrating the Jewish holiday where millions of Jews celebrate the slaughter of the first born children of Egypt.

I'll type it slower… Jews celebrating the murder of Egyptian children.

In case you're unfamiliar with the story, Moses and the Israelites were allegedly enslaved in Egypt. Often, the pious will try to blame the Pharaoh and say he refused to release the Israelite slaves, but actually God takes credit for not letting the Pharaoh free the slaves.

> *"The LORD had said to Moses, "Pharaoh will refuse to listen to you—so that my wonders may be multiplied in Egypt." Moses and Aaron performed all these wonders before Pharaoh, but the LORD hardened Pharaoh's heart, and he would not let the Israelites go out of his country." Exodus 11:9-10*

Why would God not let the Pharaoh free the Israelites? So his wonders may be multiplied in Egypt. What does that mean, exactly? It means God is going to rain the ten plagues down upon Egypt and there's nothing the Pharaoh can do about it. The Pharaoh didn't bring it upon his people, God wanted it to happen:

> *"So Moses said, "This is what the LORD says: 'About midnight I will go throughout Egypt. Every firstborn son in Egypt will die, from the firstborn son of Pharaoh, who sits on the throne, to the firstborn son of the female slave, who is at her hand mill, and all the firstborn of the cattle as well. There will be loud wailing throughout Egypt—worse than there has ever been or ever will be again." Exodus 11:4-6*

And Jesus celebrates this act of infanticide at the last supper, and even claims that Passover is celebrated in heaven. In heaven, they celebrate the slaughter of children.

> *"When the hour came, Jesus and his apostles reclined at the table. And he said to them, 'I have eagerly desired to eat this Passover with you before I suffer. For I tell you, I will not eat it again until it finds fulfillment in the kingdom of God.'" Luke 22:14-16*

The test of Job is another good example of God's morality. In the book of Job, it opens with a description of all the good things Job has: 7 sons, 3 daughters, 7000 sheep, 3000 camels, 500 oxen, and 500 she-asses and last but not least. . . the servants/slaves; household members who aren't part of the family. Then the story talks about how when any of the sons of Job celebrates a birthday, he has a banquet and invites the three sisters to eat and drink with them. Because women are so filthy and vile, Job is afraid that his sons are sinning physically with their sisters. Their sins are of the flesh, even though they love God in their hearts, so every morning after one of these parties he offers up burnt offerings to assuage their sin and wash the filth of their sisters off their souls.

Here's a quick moral insight into the evil God monster of Abraham. In God's eyes, it is good that you slit an animal's throat and then light it on fire in sacrifice to him. That's what God wants! Of course, we all know the reason Christ was 'sacrificed' was so people would no longer have to offer up such sacrifices, but still, I'm not entirely sold on that one either. As mentioned, Jesus celebrated Passover and was looking forward to celebrating it again in heaven, yet Passover very specifically requires the slaughter of a baby sheep or goat…

Ok, back to the story of Job. So, God is sitting in heaven looking down upon Earth when a group of angels comes to him. Satan is among them and God, being the all-knowing all-seeing creature he is, asks the adversary, 'Where have you come from?' and Satan replies that he's been roaming the earth, going back and forth. Then the very next line God essentially starts the game by bragging about how one of his slaves, Job, is blameless and upright. This slave fears God and shuns evil. Notice that last line? It doesn't say Job loves God or has a fuzzy notion that God is good or nice. No, it says he fears God and shuns evil. If this man Job even suspects a sin against God has been committed, he immediately offers up living creature to die a horrible death in burnt offerings. Recurring theme: Cruelty to another man/creature is a good thing in the eyes of the Lord. Of course, it could be argued whether a burnt sacrifice was offered living or dead, but I would suspect both forms took place.

Then Satan points out that the Lord blesses everything Job has or does, so, of course, his slave is going to be penitent. Then God tells the adversary to destroy the family and possessions of Lot to prove his slave will not curse his God. Sure enough, once all has been destroyed, Lot is still faithful to God. He's gone absolutely mad, but he's still faithful. Once he's done stripping himself naked and shaving himself bald, he falls to the ground and starts praising God.

That's it. The story is over and everyone goes home. From the tone of the next chapter, God was willing to leave Job pathetic and broken, because it starts out pretty much the same way as book one. God is sitting on high watching the world go by when some angels and Satan show up. God asks Satan where he came from and Satan gives the same reply. Then God asks Satan if he's considered Job.

It should be noted that Satan is usually attributed with only killing ten people in the Bible, the children of Job, and in the first book of Job God tells Satan to do whatever he wants to Job's family and property, but it never actually says Satan murdered them. Then, in book 2 when God asks if Satan has considered Job, God even boasts that Job is still faithful, 'though you (Satan) incited me (God) against him to ruin him without reason.'. So even though Satan is often blamed for their deaths, clearly God takes credit for the act itself. It would appear Satan's role was merely that of the person suggesting what horrors should befall Job. In book 2, Satan tricks God, because that's such an easy thing to do, into inflicting his most faithful slave with boils and disease. Job does what any person would do at this point, he curses the day he was born. We all know Lot didn't curse God and we all know why. Lot, even after all he had been through, was so scared shitless of God that he couldn't curse him and he said as much.

And we can't forget Abraham and the example he and God set for an immoral god. Everyone knows who Abraham is. When we say an 'Abrahamic' religion, we are referring to him. He is the guy who started it all. His name was originally Abram and he was married to a woman named Sarai. They traveled around a bit, including a trip to Egypt where he whore'd his wife out to the pharaoh. I know it sounds harsh when I say it that way but that's essentially the deal. There's a famine in his land so he packs up his family and takes them all to Egypt. The story goes... his wife Sarai, who is over sixty-five years old, is so beautiful he's afraid if people know they are married they'll kill him so they can have sex with her. I say she's sixty-five because Gen 12:4 states Abram was seventy-five when they set out from Harram and in Genesis 17 it states she's ten years his junior. They actually traveled around a bit after leaving Harram and before they went to Egypt, but for the sake of argument, we'll say she was sixty-five. She's such a GILF (Grandma I'd Like to... Fornicate) that men are going to kill him to sex her. Anyway, he comes up with this hair-brained idea to not tell anyone in Egypt they are married, but instead to say that they are brother and sister. Well, rather than being discrete it, would seem Abram paraded her down the streets because the bible says,

> **"When Abram came to Egypt, the Egyptians saw that Sarai was a very beautiful woman. And when Pharaoh's officials saw her, they praised her to Pharaoh, and she was taken into his palace. He treated Abram well for her sake, and Abram acquired sheep and cattle, male and female donkeys, male and female servants, and camels."**
> **Genesis 12:14-16**

Some of the Pharaoh's men accidentally see her and she's so stunning they seize her and take her to the Pharaoh? And the Pharaoh thinks she's so pretty he just starts giving stuff to Abram? It sounds like Abram traded his wife as a sex slave for some farm animals and human slaves. The way the story reads, the Pharaoh ends up marrying her and, since she's already married to Abram, the lord gets angry and gives this man a disease. Naturally, the Pharaoh was pretty mad when he found out the woman was already married and sent her back to Abram in disgust. Sounds like the Egyptians had the moral high ground on this one. But let's read the part where the Pharaoh gives her back.

> *"But the LORD inflicted serious diseases on Pharaoh and his household because of Abram's wife Sarai. So Pharaoh summoned Abram. 'What have you done to me?' he said. 'Why didn't you tell me she was your wife? Why did you say, 'She is my sister,' so that I took her to be my wife? Now then, here is your wife. Take her and go!' Then Pharaoh gave orders about Abram to his men, and they sent him on his way, with his wife and everything he had"* Genesis 12:17-20

The lesson here is rather than man up and defend your wife, you deny you're married to her and allow her to sex around with men and even marry them. Especially if that other man is giving you, the cuckolded husband, all kinds of riches. And here's something that's really going to get under some people's skin. . . I think Sarai infected the pharaoh with a venereal disease. She was diseased was why the pharaoh sent them away and why he let them keep all the things he had given them. You usually don't want shit back if you've given it to someone you think has the cooties. And if she did have some kind of venereal disease, there's no doubt Abram had it as well. There are many sexually transmitted diseases which have long term effects on a person's mental abilities and can cause hallucinations and other mental issues.

This could explain his delusions later in life. His sudden proclamation of, 'Hey everyone, let's cut off the ends of our dicks!' kinda screams of mental issues, but it could also have been a measure to stem the effects of an STI that was ravaging their tribe. Don't give them too much credit, though. They didn't come up with the idea on their own. It was a trick they picked up in Egypt.

A venereal disease also explains why Sarai couldn't have children. Damage done by the infection had left her barren. Oh sure, in Gen 17 when she's ninety years old she gets pregnant, but they also get their names changed to Abraham and Sarah. I think Abram died as did Sarai, both probably from syphilis or something of the like, and a younger couple was chosen to replace them.

And what about that whole Moses in the desert thing? There's a story for you. Forty years of wandering through the desert following a pillar of smoke by day or fire by night. Forty years of the same food day in and day out, and you can imagine what happens if they complain. You realize life expectancy back in those days couldn't have been much over forty, especially considering such a harsh existence. Imagine spending the remainder of your life wandering through one of the harshest deserts on the planet, eating the same food every day, constantly praying to be delivered and showering your God, whose miracles you can see being performed by your very own eyes, with praises day in and day out, and yet never reaching the promised land. They were chasing the eternal carrot on a stick. Talk about some cruelty.

No wonder he had such a hard time keeping the Israelites in check.

Chapter 17. Angels, Demons, and Jinn

"Man is certainly stark mad: he cannot make a worm, yet he will make gods by the dozen." ~Michel de Montaigne

Michel de Montaigne (1533-1592)

Angels appear throughout the Bible and perform various functions depending on the need of the story being told. They pass messages back and forth from God to man, destroy a city here and there, and are key in the slaughter of all the firstborn children of Egypt, according to the bible. Angels pretty much did all of God's heavy lifting and his dirty work here on Earth. Don't let me take any of the murderous glory due to God from his adventures in the Old Testament. On many occasion, he would personally reach out his merciful, loving hand to his people in the form of fire, earthquakes, plagues, death, etc., and rent them asunder without the aid of an angel, but the angels were usually there, trying to warn people.

Often, angels are the guys holding the signs that read, 'Repent, the end is nigh' that everyone steps over as they go about their day. When things go to shit, as they so often did back then, these nutbags just start jumping up and down claiming they were right, that they are the voice of God. Now that you're convinced, you must heed their word and give them your money, goats, firstborn child, etc. Any of the poor, unlucky survivors of one of these events might unfortunately see these whack jobs as angels who tried to warn them of God's impending rage and pen themselves a book. Angels indeed.

Occasionally, God would make a cameo appearance in the form of a cloud, or a disembodied voice, or even in the form of a man, but normally it was angels zipping about doing the thing. They usually appear in the form of a man but they're flexible. They can take the form of a man and, in the New Testament, they show up a lot in people's dreams. Oh goodie. See, nowadays when someone tells us they hear voices in their heads we lock them in a padded room. Back in antiquity, they apparently called them prophets.

Human angels are often just people in the right place at the right time. If you were a character in the bible and were hurting or in need of help and someone stopped to help you and then carried on about their day, they would end up in your story as an angel. An example would be how you get a flat tire while on your way to work and someone stops and pulls your spare from the trunk and changes the tire for you.

> *'And lo I was sitting uponeth the side of the roadeth and an angel of the Lord appeared unto me and with a twitch of his nose, the right rear tire of my 1974 Ford Gremlin was instantly repaired. Grimmy had been resurrected from the horrors of Satan's clutches and restored unto health, complete with a full tank of gas. Twas a miracle! Before the angel departed he looked at me and said, 'For God's sake watch out for nails, man."*
> *Chapter 17 - The book of Chris*

Your grandchildren would hear the story you've been telling them and by the time they are old enough to write, they've added all kinds of miracles and wonders to the story. The angel lifted the car over its head using a magic blessing and spun it around and when it was returned unto the Earth, the Gremlin had become a fiery red Ferrari. Truly a miracle indeed. Fifteen hundred years later we have people killing each other for building their houses with nails instead of screws. A new faction would arise and be praying to the almighty Ferrari and shunning the evil Gremlin and killing anyone who doubts their existence and power. And since Christ was a man nailed to something, he must be wicked and his followers must be slain. Sacrificed to the chants of, 'Die nail man!'.

I know, it sounds ridiculous, doesn't it? IT ALL sounds ridiculous. The idea of God sending angels ahead of his chosen people, either to guide them or to destroy the people and towns in their path, either way sounds ridiculous, but it's there.

> *"My angel will go ahead of you and bring you into the land of the Amorites, Hittites, Perizzites, Canaanites, Hivites, and Jebusites, and I will wipe them out."*
> *Exodus 23:23*

Hallucination angles or visions are what we get when the writer of the story has either been indulging in some form of narcotic, has had his mind eaten away by a sexually transmitted disease, or as the result of a neurological issue or trauma. The book of revelation reads as if John had just stumbled upon a heavenly cache of magic mushrooms, and Muhammad displayed characteristics commonly associated with a brain tumor, such as his headaches, sweating, imagining he could talk to angels, etc. By no means do I intend to insult anyone with brain cancer by the comparison to Muhammad and I'm certainly no doctor. In Muhammad's hallucinations, he imagined the archangel Gabrielle giving him the words to write the Quran. Or so he says, so that makes it true. Abraham was all the time talking to 'the Lord'. Twice he gave his wife away to another man and lied to that man claiming she was his sister. The first time she was returned to him by the Pharaoh of Egypt who claimed she had given him, and subsequently his household, a disease. Later, Abraham's wife can't bear him any children, probably due to the disease, so she gives him her female slave. He gets the slave pregnant but she, too, catches his STI and starts having hallucinations and seeing angels. After the disease has addled Abrahams mind, he hallucinates into existence the first covenant of the Lord and brings circumcision to the Israelites. Then, he tries to give his wife way again. Although, the person he gave her to the second time claims to have not had sex with her, yet he and his family are still rendered barren. Only by giving Abraham's wife back does the sickness lift.

Sometimes, apparently, all you had to do was show up and claim to be an agent of the Lord and start commanding folk to kill each other and that's all it would take. Throughout the book of Ezekiel, the narrator goes on about hearing the voice of the Lord. Almost every chapter starts with proclaiming the word of God came to him.

Although there is no mention in any religious text that angels literally have wings, they are often described as either flying or traveling very fast, so the people in the middle ages gave them wings in their art and stories. Not just any type of wings either, but beautiful white majestic wings. Cherubs, the guardians of the Garden of Eden, were originally large lion-like creatures and probably had wings, but they aren't angels as much as they are creatures of heaven. And in truth, they're not even that. The idea of a cherub with the bearded face of a Persian or Babylonian king and the body of a lion with wings was a direct rip off of the Lammasu and Shedu of neighboring religions.

Assyria - Portal Guardian from Nimroud. British Museum
Statue of a lion with wings and head of a bearded man.

It's only in the Christian era where cherubs became small, nearly naked little boys (clearly a Catholic thing) with bows and arrows. A winged lion with the head of a Persian or Babylonian didn't quite fit into the religious structure.

In Judaism and Christianity, angels and demons are the same things, the only difference being their zip code. Demons are often drawn artistically as hideous horned beasts with tattered bat-like wings, if they have wings at all. It's my understanding that, although it has grown into the minds of popular culture this is what demons look like, they were originally drawn as a metaphor for the evil they represented. Demons tend to have all manner of magical mental abilities and seek out all the wicked things hidden in your mind and try to make you act on them. Now, why exactly would they do that? If the goal of Lucifer and the angels who rebelled with him was to take over heaven and play God, I hardly think they'd be here wasting their time trying to make us be bad people. If Earth is God's ant farm and humans are the ants, why would he banish his arch enemy here specifically to torment us? Why punish Lucifer for wanting the throne of heaven by giving him a throne on Earth, subjects to rule over, and humans to torture? Of all the worlds of the universe God has to choose from and he chooses a place where his most favored and beloved creature, man, dwells? It's like finding a wolf killing your farm animals, so you catch it and lock in the bedroom with your children. It doesn't really make sense. The evil, murderous God and tormentor of the bible has an enemy and that enemy is. . . bad? That enemy's followers are bad? If God's an evil hump and demons are trying to lead us away from his teachings how is that bad?

And what are the jinn? Well, the western cultures might recognize the jinn from folklore as the genie of the lamp or genie in a bottle. Jinns are hot, sexy women with long blonde hair and a very cute way of saying 'Yes, Master!'.

Historically, jinns were the demons of the desert, a Persian influence before the Islamic religion became dominant. Although I use the term 'demons' here, I don't mean demons associated with the evil God monster of Abraham. They were another attempt by the intellect of man to explain why good and bad things happen. They were creatures born of fire and were neutral and could go either way as far as being helpful or hurtful towards people. Bad shit tended to happen more often back then, so they tended to have more evil undertones. The founders of Islam had a difficult time incorporating them into the religion, as you can imagine since the role of the demon was already taken, and these were creatures born of fire. They instead decided to stuff them in somewhere in the middle. They claim angels are born of air, jinn are born of fire, and man was born of clay. In the beginning, the jinn were allowed entrance into heaven, then something happens and the jinn are no longer allowed in heaven. The teachings of Islam don't give us any description or explanation as to why the jinn were suddenly banished, they just were. As with any fractured belief system, you'll find many different interpretations. Some people believe the jinn are what everyone else knows as demons, and there is a specific jinn who is the equivalent to Satan. Others believe Satan and the demons are indeed fallen angels and the jinn are a completely separate race of being in the heavenly host. They walk the earth in a realm we can't see and have little influence on our lives.

Again, Islam couldn't quite fit them in so they downgraded them from the answers to why good and bad things happen, to mere shadows and whispers. Christianity went even further to denigrate the jinn by popularizing the whimsical idea of a genie living in a bottle waiting around to grant magical wishes. Although I don't believe in the jinn any more than I do the tooth fairy, I do believe we should clone Barbara Eden.

In Genesis, you have the story of Lot who is in Sodom when two angels come visit him. The men of the town want to rape these angels and Lot offers them his two virgin daughters instead, but the townsfolk don't want them and insist on sexing the angels. There's another story of the Levite who traveled with his manservant to the town of Gibeah where an older man took them in and the townsfolk went gay sex crazy and wanted to rape the men. The old man who sheltered them offered the crowd his virgin daughter and the Levite's concubine, another young girl, but they didn't want the girls. Just like in the first story, they wanted the men. In the first story, the angels blind the attacking townsfolk and everyone gets away. In the second story, the Levite pitches his concubine out to the crowd, so the two stories end differently, but do they? In the first story, the angel blinds the crowd. In the second, the Levite does something quite horrific to satiate the crowd. Perhaps the person who wrote the story of Lot chose to say an angel blinded the raging homosexual men attacking them, rather than saying the 'angel' used a non-virgin girl as bait to distract them.

It does seem as though they are two sides of the same story. A manservant and shitty Levite who tossed his wife out to a crowd to be raped and murdered appear in the story of Lot as two angels, and Lot is the friendly old man who offers the Levite a place to sleep. The story is the same; the names were changed to protect the ignorant.

Angels, demons, jinn, and God are all pieces of the same big puzzle. Man's great quest to understand the world around them. They are seen in our dreams and hallucinations and often speak the words our inner voice has already told us. They are a plot device when a story in the Bible requires it, and the Godly explanation of those things we see out of the corner of our eye, yet aren't there upon direct observation.

Bigfoot with wings.

Chapter 18. God Hates Sex

> "We must question the story logic of having an all-knowing, all-powerful God, who creates faulty humans and then blames them for his own mistakes."
> ~Gene Roddenberry (1921-1991)

Gene Roddenberry
Photo Credit: *Larry D. Moore CC BY-SA 3.0*

I can't really claim to understand the mind of the almighty, but it would seem as though the evil God monster of Abraham has some serious psychological issues when it comes to sex. So much so that God and sex are easy fodder for comedians. As an example, here's an article I wrote in 2009:

> "I'm betting you didn't know this, but according to my little brother's wife, who cites 'reliable sources', every time you masturbate, God kills a kitten. When she broke this news to me this afternoon I immediately realized that just since Monday I've unknowingly taken out two litters of those cute little furry felines all by myself. Then the greater magnitude of the situation hit me and I realized the

world would drown if I had a tear for every kitten I've 'single-handedly' rent asunder over my lifetime. Most of them terminated with extreme prejudice, figuratively speaking.

I've always been a cat lover; they're my second favorite quadruped, so as you can imagine this news comes as quite a shock to me. Now, every time I see a Xeroxed photo of a kitten stapled to a telephone pole with the words, "Have you seen this cat?", I feel a little guilty. It's very likely I'm the reason that poor family has lost their precious pet. Was I wrong when I thought if I did it real quiet God might not notice? Guess so.

Could it be I'm the 'Jack the Ripper' of the cat world? That's not a very good comparison as Jack the Ripper doesn't have anywhere near my numbers, but I think you know what I mean. Are the souls of the countless kittens I've unwittingly mowed down over the years dragging behind me like empty beer cans tied to the back of a car?

And what if the world found out? I can see the headlines now, "Crazy Chris' Carnal Cravings Kill Cat Colonies: Populations Dwindling!" Peta would be petitioning the government to have my hands surgically removed at the wrists.

And the crux of the matter is, what did the poor cats do to God to warrant such smiting? I have this vision in my head of some cute little kitten sitting in a room, playing with a ball or some string, and

**out of nowhere this loud booming voice
says, 'Here kitty kitty', then CRUNCH!**

**Who knows? It could go something like,
'You know I hate to do this to you Fluffy,
but that Chris is such a bad bad man,'
and then CRUNCH!**

**Either way, it's bad for the cat. And what
happens when we run out of cats?
Hopefully, God will choose a creature I
don't like such as spiders.**

**The Adventures of...Christopher
Mallard"**

Ok, as I've established, God is the imaginings of men. Not
one man, but a bunch of men, in hundreds of books spanning
thousands of years. Most of the core material was written in the
Old Testament between 400 BCE and 1500 BCE. That's 2400 to
3500 years ago by a group of desert-dwelling nomads who
believed in such horrid things as:

- o Slavery

- o The subjugation of women (directly sexually
  related)

- o The mutilation of the genitals of children (directly
  sexually related)

- o Sucking the blood off the penis of a baby who has
  just had his foreskin cut off. (directly sexually
  related)

- o Sacrificing people and animals on altars of fire

- o Stoning their own children to death

- o Stoning rape victims to death (directly sexually
  related)

- Pedophilia - In times of war, when the people who wrote the books of the bible defeated another city, the men, women who had lain with men, and the male children were all slaughtered. The virgin girls were taken as spoils of war. (directly sexually related)

These are the things they taught and believed. Many people, as you can imagine given today's examples, didn't really believe at all but rather used it as a means of power, control, or wealth.

But something about sex really seems to bother the followers of the evil God monster of Abraham something fierce. Ok, so in the ancient desert when you lived in a small community, it was unsafe to have sexual relations with someone traveling through because you could become infected with a disease and wipe out your entire village. This makes sense. If you want to ensure your children are really your descendants, then keep your neighbors away from your wife. This makes sense too. But the real pox the monotheistic religions seem to take with sex is unrealistic. Other cultures, such as the Greek and their mythologies, still had a central male creator deity, but they also had lesser female deities who were beautiful and whose bodies were celebrated. A woman's role, especially of a sexual nature in some of the Pagan rites of worship, was very important.

So what's the deal? And what's up with that whole circumcision thing? What's the point in cutting off the foreskin of a male penis and why should God care if it's there or not? If man were created in the image of God, one would have to presume God had foreskin on his penis and isn't God perfect? So why would God want a person to do such a thing as cut off a part of the body and why choose the foreskin? Well, the bottom line is that circumcision was God demanding proof of your desire to have a covenant with him by cutting off part of your dick. That way, you will be forever reminded of your slavery and promise to follow God. Personally, I'd rather get a tattoo.

My Tattoo

I must admit, even though neither of my parents was Jewish, I was circumcised just after birth and have never known what's it's like to have a foreskin. As I've mentioned on more than one occasion, my penis (photos available upon request) is my favorite toy in the whole world, so apparently, I'm not missing much. I never find myself sitting around thinking, 'Damn, if only I still had my foreskin'. But something you have to wonder about is this. . . If a circumcised penis was a sign of your covenant with God, at what point during the holy ceremonies and holy gatherings did the men go around showing their dicks to each other? I mean, if you have a secret club and every member has a secret tattoo, you at least have to show your tattoo to the doorman to get into the meetings, right?

But seriously, first I'd like to say I'm grateful God just wanted the foreskin and not any of the meaty parts. Thank you ancient crazy religious nutbags for that! And I'm also glad God wasn't asking for a nose or a finger, as I would probably miss one of those and it would be much harder to hide in public. Of course, it would have made getting into all the secret Jewish meetings a little less embarrassing. I hear there are medical and sanitary reasons for having a circumcision (which is probably why the Egyptians started the practice) and would therefore probably have it done to my son unless further research sways me against, but you can bet I'd never have it done for any religious purposes.

Here is some other reasoning I found which people have used to use to justify circumcision,

> *"In some areas of Africa, there exists the belief that a newborn child has elements of both sexes. In the male body, the foreskin of the penis is considered to be the female element. In the female body, the clitoris is considered to be the male element. Hence when the adolescent is reaching puberty, these elements are removed to make the indication of sex clearer"* *~Wikipedia*

This could indicate the real reason why Abraham wanted to circumcise all the males in his tribe, so he could make sure of who was really male and who was not. With their affinity for body hair and their evidently small penises, it must have been difficult to tell a man from a woman. This might also explain the whole beard thing. It became rude to ask if you could see someone's junk, so beards became mandatory for men as a method of identification.

When you consider the Wikipedia answer, it's difficult to imagine having a hard time telling male and females apart when they're hitting puberty, especially by the time you've stripped them down far enough to see their equipment, but you'll note Abraham told his people to circumcise their children at eight days old. I suppose at that age a baby boy's penis and baby girl's parts might possibly look similar to someone not paying careful attention. The reason why they didn't wait until adolescence may have been because the children were usually married off well before. I don't know. I'm trying to reason out why a sane man would suddenly decide to command such a thing on his own people and it's not working. In my opinion, it's another pointer indicating his mind had been eaten up by some venereal disease he got from that slut Sarai.

It's unfortunate for women that the foreskin couldn't be sewn up at childhood and only undone when a man is married. Sew it up tight enough to where any time he gets an erection there is pain. Sew it to where masturbation or sexual intercourse will break the thread or the skin of the sealed up foreskin, to ensure his virginity. Then stone his ass to death if he's not a virgin on his wedding night. A little late now, but some creative thinking in this department a couple of thousand years ago may have saved women a lot of grief. Who knows? Perhaps that very suggestion had been put forth by the women of the tribe and circumcision was Abraham's answer. Yeah, doesn't seem very likely to me either, since the men tended to have multiple wives that trick would only work once. After his first wife, he would no longer have a marketable man-hymen and then where would he be? Up a creek without a man-hymen is where he'd be.

Something else that made sense back in those days is that it may have been hard to keep a good woman if she were allowed to make decisions for herself and allowed to choose another mate. He beats her, treats her like a slave, has multiple wives so she's more like cattle than a companion, and on top of that he's cutting off parts of his dick! No wonder they had to enslave their females. Otherwise, these women would have found themselves some real men. One of the things that frustrate men of the modern era is they can't be sorry, pathetic, abusive, chauvinistic assholes because their women will leave them. They don't have to put up with it anymore, but back in those days, the women didn't have any choice. The men were stronger and ruled the women, and this is reflected in the God they created. Any woman with any sense would be out of there in a heartbeat if she only had somewhere to go. And of course, had she not been programmed from birth that this was how it was supposed to be. Women have tools to get by that men don't come equipped with, and the best way to keep them from using those tools is to make them think they're dirty; Dirty filthy whores whose bodies are unclean. They soil men with their very touch.

I hate to be the one to point this out, but given the environment they lived in and the lack of bathing water, I can kind of understand the whole notion of uncleanliness. I bet the women back then could get to smelling something horrible when not properly maintained. A woman's body is a delicate little chemical laboratory, full of all manner of various girly things that need regular cleaning in order to maintain its flowery odour.

Without this regular maintenance or with the introduction of any number of infections, the smell could get quite rough. Toss in a heavy burka, weeks or months (or ever) in the desert without a bath, and the remnants of quickie sex with your husband, and I bet things could get quite ripe. Eye wateringly so. Just saying...

But it wasn't enough to degrade them and treat them like slaves, they had to go that one step further and find a legitimate reason to hurt women sexually. I can concede the sick and twisted tradition of female genital mutilation didn't originate within the Abrahamic religions, it started with the Egyptians just like male circumcision, but it didn't take long for the woman-hating pigs of the early religions to embrace it. Imagine how delighted these sadistic nutbags were when the female genital mutilation craze swept into the Middle East. Woo hoo! You can almost bet some of them wished they'd thought of it sooner so it could have found its way into the religious text and be even more sanctified.

For those of you who don't know, female genital mutilation is where they cut off the labia and remove the clitoris of little girls, usually performed just after birth but sometimes as late as the early teens, and rarely with any form of anesthesia. It's supposed to hinder a woman's sex drive and keep her from enjoying sex. In some instances, the girl's vagina is sewn shut with a small hole left for urine and menstrual blood to flow. This is to ensure her purity and as protection for her hymen. I remember hearing about the chastity belts men would put on their wives and daughters in England and Europe during the Middle Ages and I thought they were cruel. I had no idea men could be so ugly and hurtful until I heard about female circumcision. Disgusting!

It puzzles me that the ancient Egyptians would do such a thing but all those ancient cultures had their strange ways. It's no surprise the woman-hating followers of the Abrahamic religions, especially those of Muhammad, would embrace such a barbaric practice. It's also no surprise to learn that Abraham stole the idea or tradition of male circumcision from another culture, Egypt again, and jammed it into his religion of God. His wife must have really enjoyed herself some circumcised Egyptian cock and finally convinced her husband that all the men of their tribe should do it too. Seems legit.

But the female genital mutilation is so much worse than male circumcision. Imagine being a girl of around nine years old and your grandmother and mother call you into a room and then hold you down and cut off all your external sexual organs, including your clitoris, without any anesthesia and using a rusty old 'ceremonial' knife. It happens, people! Almost every day somewhere in the Middle East a little girl is being put through this torture in the name of God, tradition, and sanctity. What are you going to do about it? Well here's something you can do... go to the web and search for 'stop female sexual mutilation'. When you find a good foundation dedicated to eradicating FGM send them all the money you were going to send that nutbag televangelist.

Sex is awesome, people! The sexual oppression laid upon the backs of the people of the world is due to a few cranky old men with a bad case of the rotten crotch.

Words of wisdom. . . don't cut on your junk!

Chapter 19. Faith Healing

"In Christianity, neither morality nor religion come in contact with reality at any point." ~Friedrich Nietzsche

Friedrich Nietzsche (1844-1900)

The preacher stood praying over a young man in a wheelchair; pain and anguish clearly showing in the man's face as the mumbled prayers grew louder and louder. Hundreds of people gathered in the large tent in the sweltering heat of a Georgia summer to be healed themselves, or find salvation and healing for a loved one, and watched as the miracles abounded. The preacher's voice reached a crescendo as the spirit of God flowed through him and into the young man's ailing joints. 'I am HEALED! Thank you, Jesus!', cried the young man as he leaped from his wheelchair. He proclaimed it was a miracle and the tent exploded with cheers and cries of 'Hallelujah!'. Clearly, this is a Christian tent. Had it been a Muslim tent the descriptor 'exploded' would have had an entirely different meaning. Once the cheers died down the young man stepped aside so the preacher could continue his work. Then, once the show was over, the young man who was just healed slipped backstage, changed clothes and started taking down the set with all the other stagehands.

Do you remember the pet rock fad that came and went in the late 70s and early 80s? If you were around during those days and you had a pet rock, did you really believe it was your pet and that it had feelings? Of course not, it's just a rock. Have you heard about the nutbag televangelist John Avanzini who would go around giving people shiny stones which they were supposed to carry around with them? Yes, he gives them these stones and tells them to rub them and pray for them and God will answer their prayers. He read in the book of Judges 6, that Gideon set an offering of goat meat and bread on a rock and an angel touched the meat and bread with his staff and fire flared from the rock, consuming the meat. This somehow makes all little rocks holy if properly blessed by this dipshit. I want to call him a whack job, but the real fools are the people who fall for this crap. He also has a special method of helping you get out of debt. Send him a check equivalent to one month's rent on your home and God will shower you with prosperity. Just remember to keep rubbing your lucky rock.

These types of faith healers show up all too often in our modern world, primarily because we let them. They are nothing more than con men and they know how to spot an easy mark. People who have been led to believe fairy tales all their lives are easy to swindle for obvious reasons and are absolute fodder for these charlatans.

Con men use the victim's own god as an illusion device to fool these people time and time again. This is clearly proven by the legions of people who turn out to watch these so-called 'faith healers' work their magic. They want to believe so very badly they'll often overlook even the most poorly executed sleight of hand, just in the hopes that God will hear their prayer or heal their wounds. In many cases, to the point where they've lost their life's savings to these scumbags or worse. And these sick bastards, the ones who know they are doing wrong, don't even lose a night's sleep over it. They carry on as if they are holy and righteous and anyone who questions them is 'persecuting' them and their rights to spew this filth. It simply escapes me how so many of these guys get away with it Scott-free. If I went on the internet and offered a product that didn't work or that never arrived after purchase, I would be thrown in a jail cell and left to rot. These guys hide behind the shield of freedom of religion to propagate their chicanery.

On the other hand, you have good people all over the world, in local churches and mosques, who truly believe what they are doing is good and that they can heal the sick through God. If they pray hard enough, they can help Sally grow back her left arm. If the person wasn't healed, then clearly their faith wasn't strong enough or God simply wants them that way for his own, unknowable reasons. Often times, the people seeking help have already sought real medical treatment, but either couldn't afford the help they needed, their needs were beyond the abilities of modern science, they live too far from real medical facilities, the list goes on. As medical science and the abilities of doctors advances and the prices of their services and tools decreases, these faith healer nutbags will have no place to perform their douchebaggery. People will simply stop falling for their shit. The televangelists are the worst of the bunch, and with any luck, these horrible people will get what's due them; a long prison term. They blatantly use religion to play on the most desperate people in society, the elderly and the infirmed. And while these tormented and suffering people search for a miracle to ease their pain, these televangelist jackasses siphon their last penny without regret or remorse. When they are caught and brought to justice, their entire family and the families of all their lieutenants should be reduced to utter destitution. If those family members made their way with their own education or business venture not bought with the dirty money of the person in question, then they could keep it, but if Benny Hinn's kids, for example, start businesses with money from his enterprises, then it should all be taken away. These are the worst kind of robbers our civilization has known and they prey on the weak, poor, and infirmed, yet they are elevated nearly to the level of godhood by their believers. It's repulsive to the humanistic mind and yet they get away with it and cause so much suffering. It needs to stop.

Some people take it even further. They choose to live in misery and pain while praying to God to cure them rather than seeking real medical attention altogether. If you're a grown person and believe in God and want to risk your own life by not seeking medical attention that's one thing, but when children start dying these horrible and painful deaths by illnesses which were easily treatable, that's a completely different story.

Another perfect example of why religion is harmful. In 2009 Herbert and Catherine Schaible refused to call for medical assistance and sat by and prayed as their 2-year-old son Kent died of pneumonia. They were sentenced to ten years of probation and ordered by a judge to provide regular medical treatment for the rest of their children. In April 2013 they lost another son, 8-month-old Brandon, after once again sitting by and praying while their child died a miserable death. Although I'm a humanist, I must admit people like these are the ones who truly deserve the death penalty. They quite possibly could be beyond reason and beyond cure. You shouldn't get multiple chances to do such horrible things to your own children, but that's what faith healing and freedom of religion get you.

An unfortunate reality about our political views concerning religion means we have to give these fools their right to believe whatever batshit crazy idea comes along. So, really, it's the flaw of civilization for not throwing these two idiots in prison for the rest of their lives the first time. Or at the very least, they should have had the rest of their children taken from them forever. If such ludicrous and dangerous belief systems were not allowed to be taught then perhaps these people wouldn't have fallen into the trap of blind faith and their children would still be alive.

These televangelist scumbags get on TV and gain access to lots of fragile minds and root them further into the belief that if they send their money to this preacher, he will ask the evil God creature to heal their wounds. Is it wrong for me to suspect the religious leaders are such low, pathetic scum bags that they would actually be willing to make their millions off the backs of the poorest people society has to offer? No. Religion is a hideous bottom feeder, trolling on the poor and uneducated, and having its members indoctrinate their children at a young age.

Now I realize modern medicine isn't perfect and they have a long way to go, but look how far they've come! No one can deny the medical advances our civilization has achieved in the last fifty years alone. Most of the medical advancements from the past three hundred years were borne of the blood and tears of scientists who were persecuted and killed for their beliefs and their research.

It could be argued that there are significant medical breakthroughs currently being held back from the public because the treatment is so much more valuable than a cure. How many trillions of dollars do you think the medical industry would lose over a ten-year span if suddenly there were a five dollar pill that could cure any cancer? How much money would the oil industry lose over a ten year period if an over-unity 'free energy' device were created, small enough to power a car where you never had to buy another drop of gasoline again? Once you get those numbers soundly figured in your head, you will know why some people suspect our science is even more advanced than the general public is aware.

Wait... it's crazy for me to suspect the government, insurance companies, and medical companies would hold back vital cures and medicines for fatal diseases simply for enormous wealth and power. No one could get away with such a thing, it's just silly. No one would use business and politics to cause your loved ones to suffer and die just for money and power! That's obscene! That's just inhumane! The only thing more sick and depraved would be for religious leaders to do the same thing and for the same reasons. And guess what? Surprise! Fully sanctioned televangelists 'heal' people on live television every Sunday, while people sit and suffer and pray and refuse to go to the doctor because they've sent in every dime they have to that preacher on TV and surely that miracle will come rolling in any moment. Or, as in the case with the parents who prayed their children to death, they watch a loved one die an agonizing death while waiting for a god who doesn't come. And then they are foolish enough to do it again.

Blind adherence is a key point of faith, and that's exactly the type of mentality these people are looking for in their 'sheep', but it can't continue. We can't let it go on. The sheeple need to wake up. And the truly sad part is that many of these people are not poor, uneducated people. Don't get me wrong, I fully believe the cults of today specifically target the chattel of society, but some people who fall for this stuff are smart, reasonable individuals who have degrees and hold down jobs. It's only when it comes to God and faith that they set reason aside for the eternal greed of an afterlife. But if these people are so willing to set aside the use of reason that helped them succeed in life and willingly fall for this crap then, in my opinion, they're getting what they deserve when they hand out their hard earned cash to the carpet baggers. It's those who target the little old lady who has lost her husband and is all alone living on a tiny monthly stipend who need to rot in prison. She turns to the televangelist for help and the only thing he's willing to help her with is emptying her bank account. It's a shameful and disgusting practice that needs to stop.

Science and reason are quickly shining a light in the dark places these monsters like to hide. If only that same light of reason could be shown on our lawmakers so they'll start putting these televangelist bastards and all their minions behind bars for life, the world would truly be a better place.

And you call me, an atheist, immoral? How dare you?

Chapter 20. The Evolution of God

"You are, of course, free to interpret the Bible differently-though isn't it amazing that you have succeeded in discerning the true teachings of Christianity, while the most influential thinkers in the history of your faith failed." ~Sam Harris

Sam Harris speaking in 2010
Image Credit: Steve Jurvetson

Although many religious believers don't believe in evolution, what they do believe has. . . evolved. Originally, the reward from God for diligent service was a long life and many sheep and slaves. There was no mention of the afterlife as we know it in modern times, so when did God suddenly open up heaven to everyone?

What was God, in the beginning, and how has our civilization morphed him into what he's become today? Based on the way the original text reads, God had a limited view, a central consciousness, that could only be in one place at one time and you could do things without his knowledge. You could be somewhere and he not know where you were, or do something without his ever watchful eye upon you. Somewhere along the way, God turned into an all-the-time, everywhere being. At what point in history did God become as all-knowing as Santa Claus?

Oh yeah. I forgot about Santa Claus. Jolly ole Saint Nick is an excellent example of how you can program people to believe there is an imaginary person who knows every good or wicked thing you've done and is writing it all down in a book. Preparing to use that book against you at a later date to determine whether you're to be punished or rewarded. In fact, in atheist circles, Christ has often been referred to as the Santa Claus for grownups.

There really was a man named St. Nicholas, and through the centuries he has evolved into an all seeing, all knowing enslaver of elves, who lives at the North Pole and uses flying reindeer to bring toys to all the good little boys and girls all over the world in one night. If you just push back the reward/punishment time factor from each Christmas to the end of life, and up the ante from presents to heaven and coal to hell, and now Santa Claus is Jesus Christ.

In the beginning, there wasn't much in the way of heaven. As I mentioned, your reward from God was a long and prosperous life here on earth. That's why many of the important people of the Old Testament were reported to have lived so long. That was the author's way of telling you how holy or how much in God's favor these people were, so it would make sense they would add a few hundred years to their age. It's not much incentive to follow the doctrine when the people who were 'blessed by God' didn't live any longer than the next person, so in the retelling of the stories, the ages of the protagonists were extended posthumously. Back then, they hadn't conjured up much in the way of an afterlife per se, but they had imaginings of a God. It started with a sun god and then progressed over time to a sky god. The next logical step would be the earth god and we actually have examples of those types of faiths in the Wiccan religion. The whips and harnesses of the sky god religions stunted the expansion of the earth god religions, so they didn't quite enjoy their heyday before it was supplanted by science. The next logical step in the evolution of religion would be the worship of the man-god or science. By this, I don't mean worship of a deity wrapped up in a man's body, I mean the acceptance and appreciation for the amazing list of things man has accomplished and of which man is capable of achieving.

Religion shunned and persecuted science, but now when we bring up something such as the advent of Alternating Current electricity or the cure for polio being the work of a man, the theists try to put their God's name in there as if he supported the work. You thank God for the stem cell research that helped save your baby... Yes, that same stem cell research the religious people were claiming was an abomination in the eyes of who? God. This is the kind of duality faced by scientist today. 'You scientist are bad and evil! I trust my God! He will protect us!' and then the next thing you know, they're screaming 'Oh help me Mr. scientist!' or you're jumping in your car with its gas-powered engine, electric lights, and GPS navigation system and rush home to your all electric home. You turn on your 50" plasma television and watch some religious nutbag tell you the pursuit of worldly possessions is bad and that you need to send him your money. You pray against the evils of the technology of today, but when your child has an allergic reaction to something, you don't rush him down to your church. Well, you could, but if the child dies even most of the fellow religious members of society would question your reasoning for not taking the child to the doctor.

But don't worry. God has gone from being a cloud on a mountain or some guy in a tent, to being everywhere all the time. It's the 24 hours a day, 365 days a year God channel. All God, all the time. He's even at the hospital. People rush their sick baby into the emergency room and some nurse or doctor who has been studying medicine for years and years, pouring their life into the art of healing people, saves their child's life and who do these parents thank? God. Sometimes they will extend their fullest gratitude to the doctor, there is no doubt, but all too often their main praises go to God, while the person who actually administered the lifesaving medicine gets a passing thanks. How many actually realize that just a few hundred years ago, the people pioneering the medicines and techniques that just saved their loved one's life were being persecuted by the same brand of church they sit and worship in every Sunday? They sit in a pew and thank God for the miracle and stare up at a cross with a mostly naked Jesus nailed to it and thank him for the life of their daughter or son. The same cross and the same Jesus who as little as three hundred years ago people were praying to for guidance just before they burned the heathens, heretics, and witches at the stake for practicing witchcraft and alchemy.

And sometimes the theist will argue the knowledge and tools the doctor used were either given to him by God or were otherwise somehow God's creations. I find this insulting to all of science. They are thus taking away the credit due to thousands of tireless men and women who sacrificed so much on the altar of science; often against the will of the very God these people are trying to pitch the credit to. In my opinion, it should be shameful for a Christian to claim God had a hand in building the CT scanner used in hospitals, for example.

In the Old Testament, God showed himself in many forms. In the story of Abraham and Sarah in Genesis, the lord comes in the form of a man. Specifically not described or referred to as an angel, but described as a man referred to as the lord sitting in Abraham's tent. I've heard some argue this is actually Jesus before his birth to the Virgin Mary and they see it as proof of his divinity. Then, later in the book of Genesis, God presents himself as a giant thunderous cloud hovering over Mount Sinai. There to give his chosen people the laws they should live by, and yet he can't manage a form less terrifying to a bunch of desert nomads than a big thunderous cloud.

God clearly seems to change and be very dynamic depending on who's doing the worshipping or who's telling the story. One person thinks he's a loving God, the next person believes he's a God who should be feared, and the next thinks he wants them to kill someone in God's name. And oddly enough, they can all go to the same church or mosque and hear the same message and still find disparate meanings. This entire mentality that God is a personal experience and choice each person has to make is something of a new thing. In the past, the church preferred to dictate the relationship people had with their God because it made them easier to control. Fortunately, the rest of the world is seems to slowly be learning how religion is a bunch of crap that ends up being quite dangerous, especially when mixed with government.

The idea of religion and God are too dangerous a weapon to allow. Most of Christianity has softened over the past couple of hundred years, so had it not been for radical Islam raising its ugly head, the era of science may have come into its fruition without clashing so hard with religion. But Islam's influence has proven to be a blight on the intellect of mankind. Some kind and gentle mother may love a generous and fuzzy Allah, but when she gives that blood-soaked Quran to her children there's no telling how they're going to interpret its teachings. There's a mother of two young men who set off bombs at the Boston Marathon who should be asking herself some very hard questions right about now. Like, how could her sons have interpreted the message of Allah in such a fashion, and where she might have gone wrong? Did her faith cause this or was it something else? However, I fear as the news reports come in, she may have been a driving force in her son's radicalization. Her own faith deepening over the past few years has ended with her being a fanatic religious nutbag who is certainly guilty of indoctrinating her children with a religion of murder. Just like so many others throughout history, these people put so much stock in what an invisible man is going to do to them in the afterlife and not enough time concerned with what's going on in the real world in which we live.

A time or two I've mentioned the chemicals people release in their brains when they whip themselves into a religious frenzy. I believe there are those people in the world who are addicted to those chemicals and sit around praying and finding oneness with God, specifically so they can get their fix. They reason it out that they are communing with the lord when in reality they are doing little more than hitting the heavenly crack pipe. There's nothing quite like feeling the 'I'm so special because God loves me' chemical floating around in your brain. You keep your little crosses everywhere and an artistic picture of the Virgin Mary as the desktop background on your computer so you can bow your head at any time and get your fix. The unfortunate thing about this type of mental disorder is that it's so hard to get a clinical diagnosis on someone to tell when they cross that thin little line between a benevolent worshiper and a murderous religious fanatic.

What is your God now? Nothing more than a list of atrocities, a pit full of bodies, a trail of burned toast, and a shot of endorphins in your brain. This is what you get when you worship gods created by men who lived in the desert, sacrificed living creatures by burning them to death, raped little girls, and wiped their asses with their hands. With any luck, you've managed to look past the sardonic nature of this book and find the message that lies within. Religion is dangerous, people! There's no way you can doubt that fact. And it doesn't seem to matter how soft and fuzzy you make your God, someone will find a way to kill in his name. It's time to evolve, culturally, and banish the God of Abraham and his prophets forever. Making them nicer only lasts a little while, until the next cult comes along.

We should reason a way to put them in their place, the past.

Chapter 21. It's Been a Good Ride

"Life is no 'brief candle' to me. It is a sort of splendid torch which I have got hold of for the moment and I want to make it burn as brightly as possible." ~George Bernard Shaw

George Bernard Shaw (1856-1950)

Well, here I am in my forties, roughly halfway through my life, and I've been pretty lucky so far. Blessed, dare I say. I've made it through in reasonable health, with the exception of a bad tooth here and there. No major traumas, I haven't lost a limb or had to survive some horrible childhood disease. I've managed to have my share of fun with the ladies and never catch an STD, especially one of a terminal nature. I haven't gotten cancer, even though I used tobacco for almost forty years.

Now, barring illness and injury, I face the next forty years or so and hopeful I'll be as fortunate. My family history predicts I'm likely to have diabetes or heart disease kicking in around my 50s, but I've lead a healthier life than my parents and their siblings, and I don't smoke cigarettes, so I may get more mileage out of my body than they did theirs.

Thanks to those diligent scientists and researchers in the medical field, I may live into my 90s. The scientists are doing their part and I'm doing mine by watching what I eat and trying to exercise on a semi-regular basis. Neither of which I remember my parent's generation doing, so hopefully if I do make it to my 90s I won't be bedridden from my 70s.

> **"Never be a spectator of unfairness or stupidity. The grave will supply plenty of time for silence." ~Christopher Hitchens**

But why? Why didn't I suffer through my childhood in horrible pain? Why haven't I ever been in a horrible accident and become handicapped? Why didn't I starve to death as a child? Why are there so many people out there who believe so deeply, yet these horrible things do happen to them? I'm not even talking being murdered in the name of God or anything of the like. I'm talking about innocence wounded now, today by God. A quick internet search will find news reports of a bus full of church kids going to or from a retreat or some other function, when the bus crashes and several of them are killed and others are maimed for life. It's an unfortunate fact, but it's a fairly regular occurrence. Why? Where's God's love and protection? And don't even sicken me with your vile argument that God called them home because he wanted them in heaven. As if they are somehow so special God needs them in heaven a.s.a.p. Heaven just couldn't wait for little Bobby and little Suzy…

Even when I was a Christian I was never a very good one. There was never a time in my life as a Christian, even surrounded by the most devout group of believers, where I didn't feel awkward and embarrassed. When I went to church, the best you could get out of me was that I would take my hat off and bow my head when it was time to pray. If I was sleepy I might even close my eyes. If not, I would glance around and look to see how many other people were not really praying too. More often than not, if I was in a church during my teens or early twenties, it was because I was with some woman and she and/or her mother was big into the church so I would play along.

I've always had my doubts, as far back as I can remember. My earliest memory of doubt was when I was about three or four years old. I saw a picture in my mother's bible of Jonah and the whale. The picture showed a stout, muscular man, naked with white hair and beard being spat from a whale, with the whale's tongue wrapping up between his legs to cover his pride. When I was told the story surrounding the picture, I couldn't read at the time, none of it made any sense. God got mad at a man and made some people throw him off their boat and a whale swallowed him? Then God destroyed the boat and Jonah rode inside the whale for three days? I'm over forty years old now and it still doesn't make any sense. Masturbation being a bad thing in God's eyes was another thing that just blew my mind. I can understand having the common decency to not do it in public, but to not do it at all? Give me the most wonderful toy in the entire universe you could possibly give a man and then tell me I can't touch it? Ever? That's just sick on so many levels. You're just asking for someone to get hurt. Tell me I can't touch my pee pee and violence is going to ensue! It's mine, damn it, and I'll wash it as long as I want to. Till I think it's clean!

The human brain is an extremely complex bio-chemical computer, of that there's no doubt, and our experiences with computers have taught us that due to the sheer complexity, there is no 'exactly right' and no two are exactly the same. You can take ten brand new identical computers right out of the box and perform the simple task of timing how long it takes for each to boot up to the first screen that asks a question. Time this down to a tenth of a second and I bet no two computers will have the same time. Come on, a tenth of a second isn't that bad. I could have said a millisecond right? These are computers and they all have identical software and hardware; all ones and zeros, right? Here's a second trick, take those same ten computers and boot them up again and I bet you not a single computer has the same boot time the second time around as it did the first, to a tenth of a second. Ok, so each one boots up slightly differently, both from others and itself, every time because they are extremely complex devices. There's so very much going on inside them it's difficult for the common man to conceive. Like computers, people are extremely complicated. Even when we come from the same home and learn the same lessons, we still walk away with our own understanding of what we've learned. When were taught something as dangerous as a religion, there's no telling what the repercussions will be, but you can be assured blood will be involved.

So why do I care? What's in it for me? If I don't believe in God, why do I spend so much time and effort studying and arguing against him/it? These questions have so many answers but the main one being I don't want my children to be forced to pray to, worship, or even have to acknowledge the existence a god or gods whom I don't believe in. It's dangerous stuff.

Back when I was married to my ex-wife, we were sitting at home one day when the doorbell rang. I, my wife and son all got to the door about the same time to find a short, well-dressed man standing there, smiling. He introduced himself, told us what church he was with, and then asked if we had time to talk about Jesus. I very politely thanked him and told him we were atheist and not interested. He said he understood and then left. As the door swung closed, my ex-wife, the agnostic, said, 'Don't tell people that! They'll burn down our house!'

Now, why do you suppose she said that? He was nice, polite, well-mannered, and he didn't even freak out (externally) when he heard the word 'atheist', so what dynamics went into play to make her say what she said? Religious people have a history of violence against non-believers going back thousands of years and here we are, a family of non-believers, telling the theist at our door to go away because we don't believe. Although we never saw him again and he didn't burn down our house, the point is that religion and its followers have a notorious reputation and it's well earned. Good people of the world need to stop being afraid and start being proactive on the issue.

What about the very real threat against myself and my family for expressing my beliefs and trying to lead others from their faith? Am I worried about someone killing me? Hell yes! I've had to ask myself things like, 'if this book succeeds and I write more and eventually get the opportunity to team up with the likes of Richard Dawkins or Sam Harris to openly debate the merits of religion and god with theists throughout the world, would I have the stones? These men bravely put their face out there for the world to see, then shine the light of reason in the dark places which, unfortunately, still abound, and I almost find it a miracle to itself that they haven't been attacked or otherwise been rent asunder. I would say 'Knock on wood', but I don't believe in that stuff either. I can only imagine the hate mail they must get from the flock of the merciful and loving God. I'm just a very opinionated nerd who took it upon himself to write down his own form of batshit crazy and call it a book. I don't know if I have the testicular fortitude for such endeavors, and I certainly don't have the eloquence of speech, but someone has to make the tough sacrifices so our children and our children's children don't have to live in fear or in constant oppression and prostration. I have a running joke where, after saying something blasphemous I'll put on my redneck's voice and say something like, 'Pop pop! Take that, funny man.' It's a morbid joke implying the last words I'll hear will be from some gun loving, bible thumping fanatic who apparently doesn't like my sense of humor.

Little girls in Afghanistan get acid thrown in their faces just for going to school, so I can imagine what those folk over there would do with me if they had the chance. I certainly don't want to be the person who 'takes one for the team', but someone has to risk it. Do you know why? Because... little girls in Afghanistan get acid thrown in their faces just for going to school! This is not just one nutbag on a moped going around Kabul with a bottle of acid. No, it's a religion! It's someone's interpretation of the will of the evil God monster of Abraham and it must stop. I want to live to a ripe old age, but sometimes I don't get what I want. So, go ahead, kill me. Cheat Allah of his chance at winning my soul. Add my name to the list of 'atheist martyrs' who've given all they had for truth and reason. Prove me right. Add weight to my argument when I say the teaching of religion should be banned or outlawed, or that men of reason should separate themselves from men of faith. And if you're going to be one of those people who say atheism is a faith, I say don't be an ass, you know what I mean. Or better yet, fine! You win! It's a faith!

"What happens to the faith healer and the shaman when any poor citizen can see the full effect of drugs or surgeries,

> **administered without ceremonies or mystifications? Roughly the same thing as happens to the rainmaker when the climatologist turns up, or to the diviner from the heavens when schoolteachers get hold of elementary telescopes."**
> **~Christopher Hitchens**

Remember the chapter on anti-theism where I talked about putting prayer against doctors in a hospital? Well, we have a winner! We've found a faith system that works. One where we can take lots of dying people and have our 'mystics' heal them, trained in the arts of their faith, and have an 80-95% survival rate. We can put these mystics in any hospital and they will turn out many healthy people. And here comes the really awesome part... it doesn't matter if you believe in them or not. Of course, they still want their gold or sheep or whatever, but you don't have to pray at home or tithe every week. Swing by once a year and let them 'bless' you and wave their holy wands and equipment around you and you'll be good to go. Although I must admit, like any other blood cult, they're going to require a blood sacrifice from time to time (want to draw some blood). It doesn't hurt much and, unlike the old days, they kinda freak out if you splash it around. They're funny like that. In case you haven't seen through my thinly veiled sarcasm. . . It's science! Hospitals and doctors! It works!

> **"It works! It works, planes fly, cars drive, computers compute. If you base medicine on science you cure people, if you base the designs of planes on science they fly, if you base the design of rockets on science they reach the moon. It works. Bitches." ~Richard Dawkins**

And that's why we're angry. We're right and we have the scientific evidence to back it up. We have a million bits of evidence to your none, yet you still demand proof. For thousands of years the religions of the world have left the earth's sands red with blood and we, those of reason, call for an end to it, yet we are bad and we are considered immoral? Surprise! That makes me angry. You want to get indignant and ugly with me when I don't want your God shoved down my kid's throat at school? That makes me angry too.

It's coming, people! The collective intellect of mankind is evolving and we're not buying into your BS hocus pocus anymore. The God of Abraham and his minions are soon to be relegated to the shelf of mythology where they belong. Mankind's most damaging and dangerous mistake in his search for understanding, the evil God monster of Abraham and his prophets, will hopefully someday be banned from active worship.

> **"There is no polite way to suggest to someone that they have devoted their life to a folly." ~Daniel Dennett**

So what do you do now? You read this book and want to shun religion, so what do you do in place of your work at the soup kitchen or where do you donate food if not the church. If you're an atheist or an anti-theist and want to help, there are many ways you can get involved. Pick your cause and go for it. Search the web or your local community for secular ways to get involved. Be proactive! We are the future. We always have been.

Whether you like to admit it or not, our civilization is composed of various levels or classes, so it's understood we have rich folk, poor folk, and everyone else in the middle. Believe it or not, there are people out there from all three groups who need help. Money isn't everyone's problem and there are people from all strata of life who feel compelled to give their time, effort, and money to help their fellow man.

Rich people who give money and time are called philanthropist, people in the middle might start nonprofit organizations, and poor people even find it within themselves to donate the only thing they have, their time, and generally do volunteer work. I must admit there are countless people who do good and help others for no other reason than to try to buy their way into heaven, but there are so very many people who are just good people at their core and truly want to help others. These people seek outlets such as foundations and churches as an intermediary between the help they offer and the people who are in need of that help. They get caught in the nets of the religion as it trolls the bottom looking for the poor and weak minded to indoctrinate. These kind and earnest people get fooled into believing their goals to help others line up with the church's goals and end up becoming indoctrinated themselves. Indeed, they may believe they are helping others, but the psychological, social, and familial damage done can far outweigh the benefits of that bowl of soup. Especially, when that same indigent person and that same helpful individual could have met without the need for a dogmatic collar of mental slavery.

It's very true, there are certainly not enough secular outlets to help others in this world, but hopefully, the atheist message will spread and those good people in the church will escape their various cults and swell the ranks of the secular good. There's a place for that gray-haired grandmother whose grandson is gay and she's sick of listening to the goodly Christian's anti-gay hate speech. There's a place for that young person looking for a cause to fight for, a dream to chase, or a dragon to slay. Just seek them out.

It would be great if we could get more secular charities and foundation to adopt a clearly anti-theist agenda. Now, I'm not saying they shouldn't help the religious who may be in need, but I am saying while they're receiving the help they should be exposed to atheism and anti-theism and even offered therapy. I know, I'm asking a bit much. Perhaps we should start with posters. Also, it would be nice if the people of the United States would file a class action lawsuit against religious groups who've taken tithe unless they can prove the divinity of their god. It'll come.

> **"For small creatures such as we the vastness is bearable only through love."**
> **~Carl Sagan**

Thank you all for your time.

All Hail Megatron!

77736019R00121